Twilight

Midnight Sun:

Edward's Version of The Twilight Saga

(A Parody)

E. Cullen

Twilight Midnight Sun: Edward's Version of The Twilight Saga is a work of fiction. This is a parody of Stephenie Meyer's books of The Twilight Saga. Any names, characters, businesses, places, events or incidents, are fictitious. Any resemblance to actual persons, animals, things, living, dead, destroyed, or actual events from the past or present is purely coincidental. It was produced from the imagination of E. Cullen.

When the sun goes down, he will be clean, and after that he may eat the sacred offerings, for they are his food.

Leviticus 22:7 NIV

This confession is dedicated to my love, though she must never know that I've written about the truth…

To all who are meddlesome,

So, you're truly interested in the story of my life. That's why you're here, and I'm practically flattered. You've longed for the truth, and I've saved the best for last. I regret to inform you that I've consumed too much of my homemade red wine. You probably already know the source of my red wine. I can assure you that you can't purchase a bottle of my red wine in stores. Please forgive me if things aren't what they seem. I shall put in as much effort into this revelation as I can possibly endure during my somewhat drunken circumstance.

You may require a box of tissues with you since the truth was not meant for all to withstand. I trust you will not think any less of me as I open my heart to you. She must never know that I've written about the truth. You know exactly who she is, yet you remain. I already assume that you may smell quite nice, though we've never had the joy of coming together. I'm sure that you may one day feel my presence while you slumber. I would stare at you with temptation, yet I would not dare to go there because she would certainly sense your stench all over me. I would never do that to you though we could always gather in secret. I wouldn't mind a sample, a taste, but I'm just teasing you, so relax. I wonder where I shall begin with this confession. I could start from the end, middle, or beginning.

My hair must be perfect as I write this revelation to all. I love to check my hair every chance I get since my hair is an entity of perfection. I've been relishing my appointments at the hair salon since I always receive the royal treatment package, which is available for a limited time only. I suppose I will reminisce about old times as they flow through my beautiful mind. I will do my best to tell you as much as I care to share. Just sit back and relax. I won't harm you after you've read about the truth, though I will be tempted to fantasize about pursuing your scent. There is no doubt in my soul that your scent is terribly hard to ignore. I should probably not say anymore since you're my guest, though we are not in the same room. While you continue to endure my words as they run through your mind, do not dare to look behind you since I'm not as fast as you may believe.

You may wish it were to be, yet in reality you would probably scream at the sight of me. We shall not go there for your sake. I highly recommend that you get comfortable. Make yourself a hot cup of coffee or hot chocolate. Perhaps you would like a glass of red wine to quench your mysterious desires. You could always get a warm cup of blood, but you're not like me. You may want to become like me, yet you shall never see that day.

Drinking the red stuff for the first time is not what you think. You should always try different things at least one time in your life. I will enjoy a warm glass of the red stuff as I write about the truth. I don't mean to repel you with my cravings. You know what I am and why I drink the good stuff. You better not think that I'm a monster because I most certainly am not. I'm a leech, a junkie! I would write the truth in blood—if I could! I apologize for my rise in temperature, and I'm glad that we are not close by. I'm addicted to the red stuff. It gets us junkies high, and we love it so much. I suppose that I should get on with it since you've been perspiring for the bloody truth.

The truth was that she was a total virgin, not that there is anything wrong with that. She had never been kissed, and it was extremely awkward. When I studied her for the first time, her smell was frustrating at first, yet she remained desirable. I developed an unusual craving for her passionate red juice. When many different worlds came together, things suddenly became complicated…

Act 1

Bellduh waited for me in the dark forest as I anxiously sought her out. She had called me up earlier because she wanted to show me something unspeakable. She seemed very depressed over the phone, though I wondered what was on her beautiful mind. I was certain that she was a witch and had placed a spell on the town of Eclipse. Her and her friends were a gang of weird girls who practiced witchcraft in their free time. It was obvious that they had a lot of free time. I had made my way to the dark forest, and I could already smell her blood. The smell of Bellduh's blood illuminated my mind with extreme gluttony. Her blood was meant for my pleasure only. Only a junkie could understand the way I felt.

The rain fell hard, and the thunder erupted as the lightning lit up the sky. I knew Bellduh was across from me, but something was not right. Bellduh's blood had suddenly smelled like something foul. To be polite, it smelled like bad perfume. She hid behind a large tree and waited for me in mystery.

"Stay where you are, Edworth! Don't you dare come any closer! Just stop!" Bellduh cried.

I halted, and I didn't move another inch. I was such a sucker for Bellduh Swansinner. I really was a sucker in more ways than one. I probably would have done anything for her, but I wasn't one to keep my promises. She stayed hidden behind a large tree as my mind was helpless to think clearly.

"Bellduh, come out. Please don't play this game with me. You called me earlier, remember? Do you recall what my reason for existing is?

"So you can show everyone your perfect hair and perfect everything else?"

I have to admit that Bellduh was not the brightest girl out there, but her blood smelled great most of the time.

"Well, duh... I mean no Bellduh...That is not my reason for existing. I do appreciate the compliment, Bellduh."

Bellduh stayed where she was while I tried to think of something clever. I thought that she was really embarrassed for not remembering the reason for my existence. I felt like I was speaking to a tree trunk. All I could do was stay where I was and listen to her intoxicating voice and inhale the erotic smell of her blood, which suddenly smelled like pizza. God, I missed being normal. I hoped that she wasn't upset at me for catching me in the act as I watched inappropriate stuff on the internet. I couldn't help but enjoy all the pleasures of the internet. It's not my fault that I'm a junkie. If you happen to be a junkie, then you should understand. I continued to deal with Bellduh, yet all I wanted was her red syrup.

"You won't love me anymore, Edworth Cuddles! You won't want me anymore after you see!" Bellduh cried.

"Can you please do one thing for me, Bellduh? Please do not raise your voice to me. I can hear you from where I'm standing. Just take a deep breath and come out. Let's talk more about what is on your mind. You know that you can tell me anything."

"I will come out then, Edworth. Just remain there and promise me one thing. Promise me that you won't laugh. Promise me that we will be together, forever and ever."

"I promise, Bellduh. We will be together forever and ever."

"How long is forever for you, Edworth Cuddles?"

""Forever is forever and ever. You know what I mean."

"I hope you mean it when you say forever and ever or else!"

"Bellduh Swansinner, whether you're a witch or not, we will be together forever and ever."

"Forever and ever sounds beautiful, Edworth. Don't ever break your promise or else. Forever and ever better mean forever and ever."

The things that I've done for the love of Bellduh's blood was something that only I could do. I would have done anything and everything for Bellduh's warm red honey.

"Everything that we are is the same, Bellduh. Forever is true, and I made you that promise before. You know how I feel about your blood… I mean you, Bellduh. Remember my reason for existing. You and I are together on this one. Now please come out and show me what you wanted to show me or else I will suck you dry… I mean kiss you, like, on the lips."

The anticipation killed me with a passion inside. I just wanted to yell at Bellduh for putting me in that position. I wanted to hurt her so badly, but I couldn't do that to her. She made me miss my manicure appointment, which I was eagerly waiting for. I also wanted to try out the new nail polish glitter that was on sale.

I couldn't actually hurt Bellduh, but she could be so bothersome, even if she was actually a terrible witch. I was so protective of my sweet love, Bellduh. My attraction to Bellduh's red stuff was viciously alarming, unthinkable, and unspeakable. Bellduh's blood was mine forever, and ever. I wasn't going to let anyone have Bellduh, I mean her red polish. Her blood completed me, yet she wasn't the most beautiful person in the world, and I didn't mind if she practiced witchcraft with her weirdo friends. That explained why she and her group of friends were so weird. I desired to marry her blood, but I shall come to that later. Nothing would have torn us apart. My junkie life would have been taken from me before anyone could have destroyed our love. Bellduh finally stepped out of her concealment. Inch by inch she revealed herself to me. My mouth dropped—in disbelief.

"It's me. Don't you recognize me, Edworth? Do you still love me, Edworth? Together forever, and ever, remember?"

"Bellduh, did I really say forever, and ever?"

"Yes, Edworth Cuddles, like only one too many times and you meant it!"

I stepped back a couple of steps as Bellduh approached me. I didn't recognize her since she had aged—horribly! I was overdramatic, and I believed that I was about to throw up in my mouth, but I kept it in. I had to humor Bellduh, since all I really cared about was her blood, but I didn't want her to know that. She was capable of wicked things.

"Bellduh, you are more beautiful than I have ever seen you. You are mine, forever, and ever."

The truth was that she was absolutely hideous. She reminded me of a wicked old witch. Her lovely scent of blood was the solitary thing that kept me sane. I didn't mind that her scent was a little off that day. She looked like she had aged one-thousand years. Her hair was white, blue, and it had lost its luster. Her skin was crinkly and resembled something of a Halloween mask that I've seen in stores. I wondered where her broom was concealed. Bellduh was frail, and her teeth were almost green. Her eyes were bloodshot and teary. I noticed a tad of facial hair as Bellduh raised her arms and approached me.

"Kiss me, my love. I desire you, Edworth Cuddles. Hold me now and forever."

I cringed as Bellduh got closer and opened her mouth for a kiss. I froze up, and I didn't know what to do. I wanted to hit her with something hard to make sure that she was not going to get back up. I looked around to see if she had hidden her broom. Bellduh put her arms around me and came closer for a kiss. My arms were yet at my sides as I tilted down towards Bellduh's disgusting mouth. My eyes bulged out in fright as I drew closer to Bellduh's filth. Her mouth was slimy and grotesque. No junkie deserved to be in that position. Only a normal person would deserve to be in that situation. My face cringed in agony, and I couldn't breathe. We were about to touch tongues, unfortunately.

"NO!" I cried.

I was so relieved when I opened my strained eyes. I had let my thoughts get the best of me once more. Bellduh was grotesque, and I did not wish that occurrence on my worst enemy. I paced around my bedroom, and I wondered if I could ever be with Bellduh looking the way she did. I knew she had aged horribly, but that was just unacceptable. It was just so wrong in every way imaginable. I wanted to contact a lawyer so that I could prosecute Bellduh for causing me to have such undesirable thoughts. I consider myself royalty and consider myself to be above the rest. I don't mean to sound conceited, but I was born to be this way. I know I'm a junkie, but I want to have my cake and eat it too. Most junkies aren't like me since they help themselves to anything they can get.

The thought of Bellduh aging like a prune haunted my thoughts. All I could think about was Bellduh. I was completely obsessed with her red lava to the point that you would have lost all respect for me. Well, I guess that's what any junkie truly cared about. That's what I loved, and that's what I craved with a passion. I wanted all of her blood to the last bloody drop. I wanted to mix her red fluid with my morning coffee, yet I didn't really drink coffee. I just really loved to inhale it. I really wanted to get inside her mind. If you were a junkie like me, you would probably understand my obsession with Bellduh's red stuff. I always wanted to pour her bloody syrup into an expensive wine glass that had all kinds of fancy engravings on it. I wanted to sip it slowly and savor every treasured taste.

Act 2

The Art of Perfection

I hardly kept track of time since the only time I really cared about was Bellduh time. Ever since Bellduh Swansinner had plagued the town with her mysterious presence, everyone in the minuscule town of Eclipse had gone weird. The strange had become odder, and the dumb had become a lot dumber. I knew some people were already dumb, yet I was surprised at how much dumber they had become. I was certain that Bellduh had used her witchery on the townsfolk. I had not yet discovered that I wasn't the same. I'm a little embarrassed to tell you what Bellduh had done to me, but I will get to it later.

I prepared for school, and I always looked forward to every second of Bellduh's presence. Students had been auditioning for the Black Swan school play. I had longed to be in that play for as long as I could remember. I had my leotards ready to be worn, and I was ready to show off my moves. I loved going to school since it was a lot better than being bored at home trying to look prettier. I would have rather shown off my beauty around school, and I figured since I was a junkie that I was going to stay beautiful forever. I paced back and forth in anticipation of seeing the look on all the students at school when they watched me enter the school. I was somewhat of a celebrity at Eclipse High.

School felt like an event for me, and I wanted to satisfy everyone. I had dropped a great deal of my time relishing my own good looks. I truly had no response to why every person couldn't be equally attractive as me. It was really so sad to even think about it. I felt like I was a gift to all women, and I couldn't help but feel that way.

When I heard what the girls at school were saying about me, it was hard not to feel superior. I suppose you think I'm in love with myself. Well, maybe just a tiny little bit. Ok, I truly love myself, but you would too if you were me. I'm Edworth Cuddles, and I'm the most beautiful junkie in the town of Eclipse since sliced ham. When you're this beautiful, well, I won't say anymore because you must know the rest. It's astonishing how quickly the time can go by when you are admiring your own beauty. I'm sure you do the same thing from time to time. See, I knew it was true. You can't get through one day without looking in the mirror.

12

I love to sing in the shower as I clean every inch of my priceless figure. You must wonder what I must sing while having a long soothing shower. I always look perfect in the morning, though I don't sleep much. You must wake up as Bellduh does, with her morning eye crusts, bad hair, and foul breath. However, I don't care much for Bellduh's filth since Bellduh's flavorful red rum is what I crave to the last teaspoon with a hint of lemon juice. I always wanted to try a little lemon juice with her divine fluid.

I always prepare myself for any outing. It was time for me to prepare for school. As usual, I had planned to make my grand entrance into the school parking lot. Eclipse High was full of on and off relationships. It was especially ridiculous with my so-called family. I constantly looked forward to showing off my beautifully feathered hair. I loved to add highlights from day to day. The highlights brought out my sweet and sour eyes when there was too much sun outside. I was hot, and I knew it too much that it was almost disturbing to some. I was actually too hot at times that I had to find some shade to cool down.

It was always the same routine every single day. I believed in preserving the best entrance at school for last, and I possessed a reputation to uphold. I would arrive at the last minute to look cooler than I really was. Everyone knew me, Edworth Cuddles, the coolest student at Eclipse High.

Permit me to begin by telling you about my daily procedure. I was very cautious about my appearance before I arrived at school in the morning.

Unlike most junkies, I believed in taking care of my figure. After hours of stalking the girls in town, I spent several hours in the morning preparing for my grand entrance at school. Since I rarely slept, I had nothing better to do in a small town. I loved to practice my ballet moves as if no one was watching.

I never used to spend as much time preparing myself before school. I still take care of myself as I write, yet I'm still somewhat intoxicated from all the red wine that I've consumed. I am now obsessed with taking better care of my appearance. I exercise seven days a week to maintain my figure. I don't have to, but I want to fit in. I will start with perfecting my hair, and I happen to have the best hair in town. I make sure every hair is placed where it should be. I will use just a touch of hair gel to keep it natural looking and not glued on like some guys do. Every wave of my hair must be perfectly feathered looking. I will not leave home without perfectly feathered hair. I will not, must not, and absolutely refuse because I love my hair. I had inquired to buy insurance for my hair and was laughed at, though I didn't see what was so amusing. I've been offered cash under the table for just a handful of my lustrous hair. I'm actually better than everyone, and I know it, don't you think? Don't be upset at me, I'm Edworth Cuddles; I was born to be beautiful. I may be a junkie, but I'm not a monster.

I don't dare to imagine what people would think if they mentioned how off my hair would look on a bad day. That would just make me very upset, and give me nightmares. I hope that you wouldn't think less of me if you saw me having a bad hair day. If one hair falls out of place or if anything moves where it shouldn't, I think that I would run out into the broiling sun and hurt myself.

I didn't mean to worry you. If the weather calls for too much wind, then I will not go outside. I never went to school during bad weather since I would not want to ruin my beautiful hair. When I prepare my hair, I always use teeth whitening strips to make sure my teeth are sparkling white.

I shave my eyebrows so that I can draw them in and look sharp. I can go through a pack of whitening strips a day, and I prefer to change them every five minutes. I love to use a touch of mascara as well. I also find that since my complexion is very pale, I need a little blush to my appearance. I'm not a queer, but I really do love to doll myself up, not that there is anything wrong with that.

I will apply a touch of red lipstick to enhance what beautiful full red lips I already have. I like to add golden highlights to my hair, though the hair salon blends them in beautifully. You must think that I go too far with my morning preparation, but I say the more effort, the better. When I'm finally done with my morning routine, I look at myself. When I look at myself, all I see is flawlessness. I finish my morning routine by saying one word to myself, "Perfection." I could have loved so many girls at school, but I seemed to be in love with myself.

I gathered with my so-called family, and we were on our way to school. Being a junkie is not easy. I'm a unique junkie that does not behave like the rest of them. I miss junk food, and I still happen to enjoy the smell of it. Junk food is against junkie policy. When I drink the forbidden red stuff, I try to imagine all the sweet junk foods that I have ever tasted. I still have feelings and still miss the finer things about being normal. Though you may think I'm a monster, and I may look at you and think the same, I'm nothing but a junkie. Deep down you fantasize about me and begin to wonder. You know that you would drop everything to have what is missing in your own life. When you begin to realize that the only way to achieve this is to be what I am, you start to crave it. You start to desire it and begin to wish. You wish you were a junkie like me.

Act 3

I was about to make my grand entrance at school, though I've made my grand entrance anywhere that I went. I waited as my so-called family made their way into the school. They were a bunch of junkies that were very close to me. The first couple to walk into the school parking lot were Roosilly and Kermit. The undercover cops were roaming around the school as usual. The undercover cops were around thirty years old, yet they looked like seniors. I could smell the undercover cops as soon as they had made their first appearance at Eclipse High. Some students practiced for the upcoming auditions for the Black Swan school play. They threw themselves into the air and hovered in the air like slow motion only to crash to the ground. It was tragic to watch some of the students wound themselves. As their blood gushed out of their leotards, every junkie around them would turn around at the first scent of bloodshed. Some of the girls and boys at Eclipse High practiced their cheerleading moves as other students went around selling the bad stuff to other students. The seniors usually bullied the miners while others recorded the action for everyone's internet viewing pleasure.

Roosilly was a wannabe junkie, but she was part of my so-called family. I absolutely loathed Roosilly's attitude every time she walked through the school parking lot. She wanted to be popular so badly that she practically begged to pretend to be a junkie. She expected nothing but royalty treatment from Kermit. He always opened the door for her and treated her like a queen.

Roosilly thought she was better than everyone was, but she wasn't. Roosilly was obviously out of shape before we met. Her tight jeans didn't do her butt any justice. It seemed to hang out as she walked down the parking lot. I was embarrassed for her, but she never seemed to notice why people giggled around her. I guess it was more cushion for Kermit's pushing, if you know what I mean. Kermit happened to swing both ways, not that there is anything wrong with that. He also hiccupped a lot, yet he refused to seek help. He once had a heated romance with Casper, but I shall get into that later. I guess nobody is perfect, but I am. Roosilly walked into the school waving her newly red hair over her shoulder. She wanted to show off how perfect her hair was, but it wasn't. Not even Roosilly could compete with me in

16

the hair department. I've received phone calls from modeling agencies, but I had to decline any offer due to my busy schedule.

Roosilly wore less makeup than I did, but I wasn't embarrassed by that. I was proud of myself. Roosilly took her first step into the school and halted since she thought she was some sort of royalty at Eclipse High. She had taken her first several steps and slipped on a piece of fruit. I was embarrassed for her, yet she pretended that it never happened. I could tell that she wondered if anyone had noticed her grand entrance, and if any of the girls were jealous of her.

Roosilly hoped that people didn't notice the way her butt hung right out of her tight jeans. She wondered if any of the guys were checking her out. She had soon realized she was holding Kermit up and continued to walk. Kermit was no different than her. He wondered if any of the girls checked out his fragile body. He rarely ate anything. He was like a stick with two legs. He also wondered if any of the guys had been envious of him. Kermit wished Roosilly would hurry up as they walked. He didn't dare say it to her face. That's something I would have loved to see.

The next couple to walk through the parking lot was Alicia and Casper. Casper changed his hairstyle practically every hour. Alicia was very giddy as usual. She loved to hand out pamphlets of being vegan. She was infatuated with the vegan diet. I think that she consumed too much coffee on a daily basis. She loved to be the center of attention. She usually danced her way around the school like a crazy junkie. She had long blonde hair that stood out. Casper was totally embarrassed by Alicia's dancing and attention seeking methods. Casper was probably thinking that he wished people would stop looking in his direction as he also probably wondered if any of the guys had been checking him out. He always looked stoned out of his mind. He was recovering from a serious drug habit. Casper loved to spike his blue hair up with a lot of gel. He was very unusual, yet the girls seemed to dig him.

He wanted to taste the red honey of every person he encountered, but Casper had been under an intense vegan lifestyle, so all he did was drink apple and tomato juice. Most of us junkies were total junkie vegetarians, and there was no way that we would dare feed off any normal person. I was suspicious of him because I suspected that he had tasted the neighborhood dogs and cats. That was just so cruel.

Casper walked as if he had a large pickle up his butt. Alicia had always said what a beautiful day it was though it rarely was. She loved to be surrounded by lovely, beautiful smelling students. She was very positive as always. She had recently made the cheerleading team.

It was the moment that I had been waiting for, and I was so excited! It was my turn to make my grand entrance into the school. I had quickly put my game face on, and I made my way through the large crowd of students as they gazed at me. As soon as I made my way into the school, I had smelled the greatest thing that I have ever smelled. It was the new girl, Bellduh Swansinner. Rumors had spread as fast as a blink of an eye. The rumor was that she and her friends were into witchcraft, and it turned out that people started to believe it. They were all a bunch of weirdos, but Bellduh had something that I craved.

I had made my way into class, and as soon as I made my way to sit down, everyone was admiring my every move. Bellduh had made some new friends by the looks of it. There was that Latino girl, Angelica. She was the hairiest girl that I've ever seen. Someone should have given her girl hygiene 101. I didn't care much for her since she was not very interesting. I don't see how talking about tacos and nachos was interesting. She didn't smell good at all. She should have probably stayed away from onions and garlic. I really hated the smell of garlic. It won't kill me or anything, I just hate the smell of it. Angelica was like the girl that could never get popular if she tried. She was easily forgotten by others.

If you dislike junkies, rub garlic on yourself. We will stay away from you. Garlic is just so smelly! I sound like a child, but I can't help it when I speak of garlic. If and when you ever become a junkie, you might understand how I feel about garlic.

On to the next girl, Jessy. She had nice short blonde hair with red highlights. She wore braces, though it was very cute on her. I enjoyed every moment of her conversation since she amused me. She smelled pretty decent, but her scent was no match compared to Bellduh's special scent. I appreciated Jessy's gaze at me because she must have thought that I was like totally beautiful. The truth was that I was too good for any girl at Eclipse High. Bellduh was an exception to that. I wasn't too good for her warm beautiful blood.

I was just for their viewing pleasure on a daily basis. Jessy was probably wondering if I bathed myself every night, surrounded by candlelight. The new girl, Bellduh, was different. I felt her eyes burning a hole right through me. I almost told her to stop since it had become too intense.

I couldn't seem to read Bellduh's lips at first, though I tried very hard. I was sure that she may have put a curse on me since I wasn't really myself. Her witchcraft was irritating everyone's way of life. She wore some sort of smelly necklace that must have kept away junkies, but I could tolerate it most of the time.

I tried to imagine her thoughts, but I imagined it was full of blue skies, with pigs flying in the sky. The mind works in mysterious ways. I could only suspect Bellduh was a witch at the time. I was going to find out if it was true or not. I wanted to catch her in the act of practicing her witchcraft. I didn't want her to put me under a spell. Not all witches were grotesque, yet most of them were hideous in the town of Eclipse.

The cafeteria was full of craziness that day. The food fights were out of control. The Black Swan club had been practicing their moves as I admired them. I went to take my seat, and Bellduh was still glancing in my direction.

I was dying to ask her if she was a witch. I wondered if I would end up burning her body to a crisp as they did back in the old days. I would have done that after I finished sucking out her beautiful red lava. Junkies were known to really hate witches.

Not only did Bellduh smell bloody delicious, but she had this power over me. I felt like she was emasculating me. I wondered if she was looking at me because of my beauty or because she knew that I was trying to find out about her mysterious ways. I was going to investigate as soon as possible.

I watched many detective shows to learn how to investigate. Television could be very educational sometimes. It was going to be hard to talk to Bellduh since I was weak around her perfectly smelling blood. My so-called family had also noticed her scent, but I made sure to keep them away.

Judging by the way Casper looked at Bellduh, I could tell that he thought very dirty birdy thoughts about Bellduh. He wanted to taste her, as well as her friends. He also wanted to have pleasurable experiences with her and her friends. Casper had a sick imagination, but I didn't blame him. Some people could smell very enticing.

Alicia tried to calm him down. She told him that he wouldn't harm anyone if he only thought about tomato juice. Another way that she helped calm Casper down was when she told him to think of onions and dirty socks.

Casper smiled and thanked her for the idea. I told my so-called family that I was going to get to the bottom of the mysterious Bellduh. I couldn't take my eyes off Bellduh.

Jessy soon noticed that I was burning a hole into Bellduh with my beautiful eyes, and alerted Bellduh. Bellduh slowly looked in my direction, and I casually looked away. The moment was very awkward.

Angelica was no longer talking about tacos and nachos. I read her lips very well. She was talking about peanut butter and strawberry jam. I didn't know what was up with that girl. I wished that she would let me have a taste of her red rum since I was so curious.

Kermit and Roosilly advised against socializing with Bellduh. They wanted me to continue with my Bible studies, though I wasn't fond of Bible study. My so-called family tried to keep well-balanced by reading the Bible. They wanted me to stay clear of Bellduh since they were worried that I could catch something unsanitary. Casper agreed that it was not a good idea unless we could be safe from her spells. I told them that I would only question her, and not get involved with her.

Alicia knew that if I decided to socialize with Bellduh, it would have led to the worst drama that Eclipse High had ever encountered. I was also up for the challenge since Bellduh's red wine was worth a taste.

Act 4

I sat in Biology class and wondered if Bellduh would be in at least one of my classes. She wasn't in my food prep class, which was a lot of fun making tacos and cheesecake. I wanted Bellduh to be in my class, but it was likely better that she remained out. Her blood was lethal to my soul.

I wanted the sweet smell of her expensive red wine to blow right in my facial expression. I welcomed danger, though danger was not my middle name. I looked around me, and all I saw were students with blood that was not very appetizing. Perhaps if everyone consumed sweet strawberry milkshakes, they would have received a sweeter smelling blood. It just wasn't my day since nothing seemed to be going the way that I wanted them to. Michael Angelo Shakespeare Knewton walked into the classroom and acted out like a complete fool. I was certain that he was under Bellduh's spell that turned the town of Eclipse into a strange place. I'm pretty sure he thought about Bellduh. I could just tell what people were thinking. He probably thought about putting whipped cream and chocolate syrup all over her body and wanted to lick it up. He probably also had a fetish that bothered me. He must have desired to tie Bellduh up and force her hair back, as he whipped her behind and got to her to shout who her daddy was. I wanted to show him who his daddy was, and maybe he would have been frightened.

I always thought Michael Angelo Shakespeare Knewton was a decent person until Bellduh came to town. Ever since Bellduh arrived, she seemed to bring out the worst in people. I vowed never to allow Michael Angelo Shakespeare Knewton ever to have a chance with Bellduh.

Bellduh deserved better. He was one sick person. He was a total weirdo. He spoke in poems, riddles, and rhymes. He bragged about his dirty movie collection. He owned such titles such as Inside Hairy Debbie, Up Yours, Sensational Cherry, Junkie Wannabees, Muffin Tip Tops, and Long Hard Things, not to mention other titles that I should not mention. He had a huge appetite for his fetishes. His laugh was very irritating, and I saw him glancing over at me as I gazed at him trying to intimidate him. He didn't like me at all, and there was nothing I could do to make him like me. He knew I was a junkie, and that was that.

Another reason Michael Angelo Shakespeare Knewton disliked me was because he thought I was gay. He had a problem with homosexuality. His thoughts about me were probably disturbing. He probably thought that just because I wore a lot of makeup that I must have been gay. He must have thought that I was so pretty that it must have been true. He was very ignorant, and he had no idea how straight I really was. He was uncomfortable around me, and he wished that my so-called family and I would leave Eclipse. I wasn't about to go anywhere anytime soon. I wasn't going anywhere as long as Bellduh was alive.

Anyone who tried to sit next to me was rejected by me. I really couldn't stand the smell of someone sitting right next to me. I politely told them to sit somewhere else, and that the seat next to me was taken.

I couldn't believe it when Bellduh Swansinner made her way into the classroom, and she walked towards me. Good Lord, I wondered why she smelled so addictive. Words couldn't really do justice at how delicious Bellduh's red stuff smelled. Her blood smelled like sweet apple pie and vanilla ice cream, but it was a lot more than that. It was a very intense smell. Her scent could oddly change, which may have depended on what she ate. Witches shouldn't have smelled that good. I wasn't sure if Bellduh was a witch, but I had my suspicions. Michael Angelo Shakespeare Knewton had interrupted Bellduh before she was barely able to take several more steps. I was certain that he had snorted drugs since he had white power on his nostrils and sniffed his nose constantly. His eyes were usually bloodshot. He was certainly as high as the sky. As I listened to him converse with Bellduh, I was so certain that Bellduh had cursed the town of Eclipse with her spells.

"Where art thou now, Oklahoma? How are thy enjoying thou town Eclipse?"

"Like, I'm not liking the bum weather, Michael Angelo Shakespeare Knewton. How about you?"

"Come to art thy neighbor, Bellduh Swansinner. To be shy or to be with me. Where art to be mine, Bellduh. For do not have thy fruit, for thou art be thy danger. Roses to be thou red. Thy shall be with thou Bellduh Swansinner."

"Yea, I... uh, I'm going to go take my seat, Michael Angelo Shakespeare Knewton. Talk to you later."

"We cross thy Bellduh again."

I told you Michael Angelo Shakespeare Knewton was strange, and he had many more riddles, and poems to share, but that was another time. Bellduh continued to make her way down, and looked right at me as I pretended to cough. It was probably better not to cover my nose since it probably looked very rude to do that. I kept coughing until I could get a hold of myself. Bellduh sat down beside me as I gazed at her. I had to act fast and decided to speak to her. I was so nervous.

"Alo... I am Edwo... rth...Cuddles, you are Bellduh... Swansinner."

"Are you ok? Do you speak English?" Bellduh asked.

"Thanks for asking, I'm fine. Just choked on my bubble gum."

"I just came back from gym class," Bellduh said.

"You're supposed to shower right after," I said.

Wow. I couldn't believe that I had just said that. I guessed her blood that smelled so good was just too much for me to handle. I didn't know how to talk to her. Bellduh started to smell herself, and looked away from me. This was an embarrassing moment.

"We never really met. I've seen you around. I'm Edworth Cuddles."

"Nice to meet you, I guess. Wait, you already introduced yourself."

This was not looking good at that moment. I needed to do something fast. I was Edworth Cuddles, and I could do anything. I wanted to try to make her laugh. The girls loved funny guys, but I was a junkie. I wanted to try to be a funny junkie.

The teacher interrupted the class and started to talk about onions and carrots, or something ridiculous like that. Bellduh and I carried on a meaningful conversation.

"I really don't like onions; they stink like garbage," I said.

"I really like the blonde highlights in your hair," Bellduh said.

Wow. Bellduh actually noticed my hair. This was a breakthrough, and my strange confidence went up 1000%.

"I can spend hours on my hair every morning. I'm very conceited and so are my family members, if you haven't already noticed."

"Well, at least you take care of yourself. That is nothing to be ashamed about. I like my guys conceited and prettier than me. It brings up my self-confidence, if I date someone better looking than me."

"Whatever makes you happy, makes me happy, Bellduh. To tell you the truth, you smell beautiful. I can't get over that perfume you are wearing."

"I don't wear perfume, so I guess it comes naturally."

She had gotten that right. Bellduh's blood came natural to me, and I had planned to suck the life right out of her someday.

"So, that guy Casper. He is like so weird. Some people say he is on drugs. He looks like he's stoned out of his mind all the time."

"Well, he is my distant cousin. Casper may look high, but he is actually far from it. He can be a little off sometimes, well, maybe a lot. My family can be really weird."

"But isn't he dating your sister?"

"Well, Alicia is adopted. It's complicated. My family are junkies if you know what I mean."

"I heard you like to hang out at La Shove Me."

"Well, I don't know about that, Bellduh. I really don't want to get shoved around. I heard a lot of people get shoved around there."

"I see, well, I might go there someday, but I might be too scared. Well, this lesson about onions is making me very thirsty," Bellduh said.

I continued to stare at Bellduh and watch her talk about onions and carrots or whatever; I wasn't really listening to her. I inhaled her bloody scent, and it gives me a real high.

"Your eyes are really grotesque. They changed colors just now. Wow. That's like so weird, Edworth. They just went from green to blue, to red, to orange, to yellow, and to golden light brown honeydew. How did that happen?"

"It's like kind of uh… well, the onion, it..." I murmured.

I got up and stormed out of the classroom.I was so embarrassed that my mechanical color contacts had malfunctioned. I paid big money to have them installed.

Act 5

Dating The Junkie

The town of Eclipse had a carnival just outside Eclipse High. The carnival brought out the town nut jobs, but I was still suspicious that Bellduh had something to with it. Everyone headed over to the carnival, which was only several steps away from the school parking lot. As I stood outside at my car, I did my best to look cool. I attempted to strike a pose, and hoped that Bellduh noticed me staring at her. I pulled out a cigar, yet I didn't even smoke, but I thought I would look cool. I had a feeling that Bellduh thought smoking was cool. I felt like a movie star as people noticed me as they made their way to the carnival. I noticed Casper from where I am standing, and he was juggling some apples, yet he really sucked. I supposed that he was in the carnival spirit.

Alicia didn`t think that I should stalk Bellduh, but I never listened. I could smell Bellduh from where I stood, and she smelled like blueberry cotton candy. She stood with her wicked friends across the parking lot from me. I could have sworn that they had been casting spells on people. They were dressed up for the carnival. They looked very gothic with their dark clothing. Michael Angelo Shakespeare Knewton approached Bellduh as I watched, and actually looked forward to his poetic personality. I gave up trying to impress Bellduh and walked closer as I pretended to socialize with the others, but I listened in on the conversation. Bellduh and her friends giggled as Michael Angelo Shakespeare Knewton approached her.

I couldn't help but smile since I was ready to be entertained by his ridiculous personality.

"Michael Angelo Shakespeare Knewton, we were just on our way to the carnival, but you can come if you want," Bellduh said.

"Come thy Bellduh, shall we travel to the place be far? The roses walk but a pink cotton and the sky shall fall upon us. Will thy Bellduh accompany to thy theater for thy Opera show?"

"Gee, Michael Angelo Shakespeare Knewton. I'm not sure. I kind of have plans with, like, babysitting my dog. I might be shaving my cat. It's like a ritual of mine. I'm not really wicked witch as you may have heard. I just like practicing cool stuff."

"I shall come once more to seek thy Bellduh up this day. Seek not what is in your soul, but beware the demon is upon, who lurks thy very grounds. Take thy apple and thy rose, for they shall provide sanctuary from thy junkie nearby."

Michael Angelo Shakespeare Knewton walked away from Bellduh as I kept my hand over my mouth as a giggled. Bellduh and her friends watched as he mumbled away. I was certain he was referring to me as he spoke his riddles.

I followed Bellduh to the carnival as she walked beautifully with her friends. I savored the taste of Bellduh's blood as the air blew the scent up my nostrils. I occasionally glanced at Bellduh, and wanted to rip her clothes off, I mean, I wanted to hand her roses and a box of chocolates with the assorted flavored creams inside.

I've thought about covering Bellduh with chocolate syrup with a hint of her blood, and wanted to lick it off her body. I hope you don't think less of me, but I'm a junkie that must have what I desire. I apologize to you since I've gone too far thinking about Bellduh with my dirty birdy thoughts, yet you wanted to know.

I wanted to put an end to Michael Angelo Shakespeare Knewton. As ridiculous as he was, I hated when he conversed with Bellduh because it made my amazing mind go crazy, though I didn't show it. He had suddenly manned up and walked towards Bellduh. He wanted to ask her out on a date. He was hoping to score with Bellduh that weekend. Bellduh saw Michael Angelo Shakespeare Knewton approaching as I looked on. Bellduh saw me in the background as I continued to strike a pose.

Bellduh looked at me and smirked. I wondered if she thought that I looked funny. Michael Angelo Shakespeare Knewton noticed Bellduh`s glance at me and turned back to look back at me. He was suspicious, and he was wondering if Bellduh and I had something going on, and he didn`t think that I was right for Bellduh. He thought he could pick her up, yet he had no game.

"Bellduh, it is I, Michael Angelo Shakespeare Knewton, remember? But, of course, you do."

"Yes, Michael Angelo Shakespeare Knewton Shakespeare… Knewton. I know you. We have been around each other. How could I forget?" Bellduh said.

"Where are thou art, Bellduh? You look really, uh... nice today Bellduh. You smell good, like strawberries."

Michael Angelo Shakespeare Knewton must have smelled the same thing that I smelled, but he was not a junkie like me that was for sure. He was so pathetic. His conversation with Bellduh had gotten cheesier.

"Strawberries. Really? Honestly, I hate strawberries. I`m allergic to strawberries. They make me puke. I had a bad experience with strawberries as a child. In fact, I hate that you even mentioned strawberries," Bellduh said.

That actually made my day. Michael Angelo Shakespeare Knewton's mouth dropped. Thanks to him, I knew that Bellduh didn`t even like strawberries. Michael Angelo Shakespeare Knewton was speechless. He cleared his throat.

"I... I`m, uh, sorry Bellduh. Where art thou strawberries? I didn`t know. Hey, like, you know what? You actually don`t smell like straw... I mean berries. You know, the red... berry. Well, you smell good, like, clean. You smell like bacon."

"Bacon? Do I smell like bacon? Well, I love that smell. Michael Angelo Shakespeare Knewton that`s so thoughtful of you to say," Bellduh smiled.

Michael Angelo Shakespeare Knewton was scoring points. This wasn't right. Bellduh was not even noticing me as I tried to look cool, striking a pose.

"Where art go out with thy Bellduh? We should go out sometime, Bellduh. Like maybe... a movie? Eat popcorn, with lots of butter?"

"I don`t know. Popcorn, butter? I hate the smell. Smells like dirty socks. Movies? Sounds like a crowded place," Bellduh said.

I could hear every word from Bellduh`s mouth. Michael Angelo Shakespeare Knewton was just having such a hard time getting a date with Bellduh.

"Hey, that`s ok... I guess. Like, Where art fail? Would you like to go to the circus freak show? You know, freak show. With... like, me? Like, you know, getting drunk. Like, with me. Like, dancing like nobody is watching. If you want to, I mean, if like you don`t want to, it`s ok, I totally understand. Where art thou, right? So, do you want to go with me, Bellduh?"

"I don`t know Michael Angelo Shakespeare Knewton. Circus freak show, getting drunk? I`m not much of a junkie. I`m allergic to alcohol. Sounds a little crowded. I don`t know."

"Well, really, it`s not a problem you know. Where art thou, right? We can just hang out, like at school, like we do now. You know. Hang out, with like, me? You know what I mean, Bellduh? Hang out. No? Yes? Maybe?"

Bellduh suddenly noticed me in the background, looking all cool. She smirked as she glanced at me. Michael Angelo Shakespeare Knewton turned around again to look at me.

"Uh… Michael Angelo, Shakespeare Knewton, that`s so very kind of you. Sure, we can hang out you know. Like, as friends. I`m kind of busy these days you know. Schoolwork and stuff. You know."

"Oh, Sure. Like, no problem. We can do that, Bellduh. Where art thou, Bellduh? We can hang out as like friends and stuff. If that`s what you're into, sure. Why not? Sounds like a plan. You know, with like, me. So, I see that Edworth Cuddles guy sure has his eyes on you."

"Does he? Gee, I haven`t noticed."

"Yes, he is a real stalker, Bellduh. Well, I guess I will get back there, and let you study. Watch out for that Cuddles guy. Gives me the creeps you know. Like, creepy guy. A real creeper that Edworth Cuddles. Well, where art thou, Bellduh? Right?"

Michael Angelo Shakespeare Knewton walked back to his buddies. He looked at me with a slightly dirty look, and I smiled at him. Bellduh glanced over at me. She smiled and got back to her study book. I continued to stand and stare at Bellduh. Casper wanted to end Bellduh. He thought he would be doing me a favor, but I disagreed. Bellduh pretended to socialize, but I could tell she was just standing there, glancing over at me, pretending as if she was occupied. She seemed to be studying me. I was studying her as well, and I took notes.

It was a staring contest. A battle between sexes as I stared at Bellduh, and she stared at me. Suddenly, my concentration was broken. I saw a skateboarder approaching, and it looked like he was out of control.

Styler had just learned to skateboard and has been told before not to speed while skateboarding. He`s been drinking. After a dozen beers and smoking up, he was totally wasted. He was heading towards Bellduh! Casper saw what was about to happen. He wanted

Styler to hit Bellduh and end her. I needed to save Bellduh. Bellduh would know that I was a junkie if I saved her, unless she already knew.

Styler was about to hit Bellduh. I decided to see what would happen. He smashed into Bellduh as everyone watched and laughed. Bellduh fell back and looked at me. I put on my serious game face and looked at her. I was actually striking a pose as I looked at Bellduh. I hoped that I looked cool enough for her.

"That was… like, too late. Thanks, Edworth. Thanks for letting Styler crash right into me," Bellduh said.

"I tried to save your life. I hope you're going to make it, Bellduh."

"Your hair, it`s so… perfect."

"I spend hours on my hair every day."

"Wow. You are so like into yourself. There is something about you. Are you wearing makeup?" Bellduh asked.

"Is this an interrogation? Are you a cop? I just tried to save your life. You owe me big time, Bellduh. Don`t forget who your daddy is," I said.

"I don`t know how to thank you, Edworth."

"You smell good, like burnt bacon," I said.

"Weird… that`s not the first time I heard that today."

We both got up, and everybody at school started to crowd around us.

"It`s ok people, nothing to see here," I said.

Styler was stoned out of his mind.

"Bellduh, I`m so stoned! Are you ok? I didn`t mean it, Bellduh! Bellduh, I am stoned! Did I mention how stoned I am?" Styler said. I walked away from the scene as Bellduh was checked out.

Act 6

Instead of playing video games all night, I discovered a new way to pass my time. I loved to stalk Bellduh as she slept. She didn't always smell good. There were times that she smelled like burnt toast. I guess she had a lot of gas. Her room was filled with suspicious-looking dolls that resembled many students at Eclipse High. I thought that was so strange. Some of them had looked like they had been tortured with needles stabbed into them. One of the dolls looked just like me though my hair was a lot better. I didn't like how Bellduh's cat stared at me while I craved Bellduh. Her sweet scent led me directly to her home, though I don`t mean to sound like a pervert, but I just couldn`t help it. I would always sneak into her bedroom window. I watched Bellduh as she snored beautifully every night.

My family didn't know about my nightly outings, and I didn't intend on telling them where I went. Her room was filled with that sweet rosy smell and all kinds of witchery. Bellduh was having a dream as she whispered funny things in her sleep. She mentioned something about camels and dogs. I suppose she was into that sort of stuff.

Now she began talking about me in her sleep as I watched. I brought a bag of candy sometimes so that I could enjoy the show. I wasn't supposed to candy, but I missed it so much. Eating candy was against junkie policy. Bellduh took her hands and placed it down in her private area. She said my name repeatedly and seemed to be rubbing herself. She also mentioned Michael Angelo Shakespeare Knewton's name. I supposed that she secretly admired his poetry. She called out his name repeatedly. Bellduh was kind of a dirty girl when she fantasized. She attempted to ask me to put caramel syrup all over her body, and wanted me to lick it up. She would switch back and forth with names. I approached her bed and removed the bed sheets from Bellduh. I love how she slept in the nude. Her muffins were very ample, and her skin was smooth. She was deep into her midnight dream, and it was as if she would never awaken. I still wondered why she called out Michael Angelo Shakespeare Knewton's name. Bellduh was fascinating as she slept. I placed my face all over her body and inhaled her overpowering scent.

Act 7

The Ugly Truth

Enough was enough, so Bellduh followed me to the mysterious green forest. This was going to be a showdown between us. As Bellduh followed, she tripped. That was so embarrassing since everyone nearby watched. Bellduh was so clumsy, and she could be such a dumbsky. As we walked into the forest, we made our way to a deep part where we could not be seen or heard. I planned to hurt Bellduh, and I looked forward to sucking the red honey right out of her. We were face to face, and it was about high noon, and the sun was not shining. That moment was going to be a truth or dare moment.

"Bellduh, if you aren`t as dumb as you look, you will stay away from me," I said.

"You are the one that is obsessed with me," Bellduh said.

"I`ve been sneaking into your bedroom at night and watching you talk to yourself."

I wanted to tell Bellduh that I watched her play with herself while calling my name and others. I wanted to tell her that she sounded like such a dirty birdy, but I didn't have the heart.

"Well, like, what were you doing in my bedroom? How did you manage to sneak into my room? Do you want me to call the cops? You are such a pervert, Edworth."

"I must admit; I have this crush on you. You smell like something perfect. You mostly smell like strawberries. You can have this sweet smell of lollipops. I can`t help it, Bellduh. I can`t seem to keep away from you."

"Well, you are pretty hot. You sneak into my room at night. Next time you plan on breaking into my room, bring like a bulletproof vest. Don't make me put a spell on you. I want to be notified in advance that you are dropping by. Like, you can`t just walk in whenever you please. I happen to like my privacy."

"I was going to hurt you, but I changed my mind."

"You're not like other guys. What are you?"

"What do you think I am? Take a weird guess."

"I`m afraid to say it. You might hurt me if I say the truth."

"I will give you a clue. I'm like a crazy person."

"Are you from the mental hospital?"

"Try harder. Keep guessing until you get it right."

"Are you Batman? A werewolf? An angel? Are you a pirate? Are you a drug dealer? A demon? Spiderman? What are you, Edworth?"

Bellduh wasn't the brightest witch in the West, but her red poison filled me with joy. I felt bad for her.

"I will give you another clue. I love to suck on the red stuff."

Bellduh's mouth dropped, and she looked shocked.

"Are you… Frankenstein?"

"Wow. Do I look like Frankenstein?"

"What? You mean you're not Frankenstein? I don't get it, Edworth. What are you?"

"I will give you another clue. I'm like Dracula."

"You're not like Dracula. Where is your cape?

I was surprised Bellduh was not blonde.

"I'm a junkie!" I shouted.

"No way in hell you're a junkie! I don't believe it! You are a liar!"

I move around so abnormally and tear up the trees. I rip the trees right out of the ground with the roots out.

"Can a junkie do all this?"

"Like, what the hell? You just damaged the trees! Are you crazy? A junkie can't rip trees out, but Superman can!"

"Oh, sorry! I didn't know you were into green peace. I promise I will plant the trees back just for you, Bellduh."

"You better. What kind of junkie rips trees out of the ground and moves super-fast?"

"A super-fast and super strong one? I guess I`m an unusual junkie. I also glow in the dark and sparkle. It`s really neat. I should show you someday."

"So you are one of them."

"Say it, Bellduh. I want you to say it. Say junkie right now. I want to hear you say it. Say it like you mean it."

"Junkie! Junkie! Junkie!"

"You said junkie. How does it feel Bellduh?

"You're a junkie!"

"I hope you don`t mind."

"You must be old. How old are you? Tell me the truth, Edworth."

"I look much younger than I am."

"Wow. I heard junkies never age."

"I have been this young for over one hundred years, Bellduh."

"Well, you should stay the hell away from me then. I heard junkies carry sexually transmitted diseases."

"Not all junkies carry sexually transmitted diseases. I once had slurpeeze, but it cleared up fast. Junkies don`t usually get diseases. It`s rare, and I haven`t gotten anything ever since. I promise I won`t contaminate you. We could date and be disease free. Have you ever considered becoming a junkie, Bellduh?"

"A junkie? You have to be shitting me! Where do I register to become a junkie?"

I really thought Bellduh had been living under a rock for the past eighteen and a half years of her life. Why would she think that you would have to register? It was such an insult to my kind. Bellduh smelled like sweet cotton candy, and I couldn't seem to stay away from her. I decided to be nice to Bellduh since I didn't want her to put a curse on me.

"You register with me, of course. All you have to do is ask, and you shall receive, Bellduh. I have a question for you now. Are you a witch?"

"I… like, study witchcraft, but I'm no witch. Don't worry, Edworth. I won't put a curse on you as long as you don't piss me off."

"Well, that's good to know, Bellduh. However, studying witchcraft and putting spells on people make you a witch."

"That is like so cool, Edworth. I always wanted to become a junkie. If I change my mind, though, I will unregister."

There was no way that Bellduh could be that dumb.

"Bellduh, have you been drinking while at school today? Have you been smoking weed?"

"Uh… no. Why do you ask? You're a silly junkie, Edworth."

"I was just wondering how much you really know about junkies, Bellduh. I thought witches were supposed to be smart."

"I'm not a witch; I swear. I just like to practice witchcraft with my friends and put curses on people."

"Well, Bellduh, the truth is that I'm not really a junkie. I just like to suck the life out of people and move like Superman because junkies don't move that fast. I also like to sprinkle sparkles on myself to trick people into thinking that I'm a sparkling junkie."

"I knew you weren't a junkie, Edworth. You're just some sort of junkie, but that's cool with me. I will try not to put a spell on you. The truth is that my friends and I have already put a spell on most of the town."

I knew it. That's the only reason the town was so weird, but there was not much I could do. I loved Bellduh's blood; I mean I loved Bellduh too much to stop her.

Act 8

Meet The Parent

When I finally had the opportunity to meet Bellduh's dad, I was excited since I wondered if his blood was as sweet smelling as hers. His name was Mr. Charsleeze Swansinner. He was the town's stand-up comedian and also the town drunk. He was a retired dogcatcher and had made a side living doing stand-up comedy around the town bars. Bellduh's mother was living on the streets, but no one cared about her. I stood in the living room waiting for his arrival as Bellduh stood by my side. I could hear him walking down the stairs. Bellduh looked at me with a nervous smile. I could hear him whistling as he made his way down the stairs. He took his sweet time. He looked at me with a straight face.

Mr. Swansinner wanted nothing more than to point his shotgun in my face and pull the trigger. He was very observant as he noticed how perfect my hair was. I smiled as he looked at me. He must have thought that my hair was much better than his own daughter's hair, although he thought I wore a little too much makeup. He thought I belonged in a circus, which was not such a bad idea since it would have been fun. He couldn't believe that his daughter was involved with such a pretty boy. Mr. Swansinner believed that I was too good for Bellduh and that I could do much better. He wanted me for himself. Mr. Swansinner swung both ways.

Even though he wanted to hurt me, he felt that he could trust me with Bellduh, since he thought that I looked gay. He thought that Bellduh could kick my ass. He approached me and offered a handshake. He wanted me to feel his hard grip to show me who was boss, though I could have easily crushed his hand in an instant, but I wouldn't have actually done it. Could you imagine the look on Bellduh`s face, or even her father`s face if I had crushed his hand? It would have been priceless, and somewhat funny to me, but Bellduh would not have appreciated it, and her father would have been in agony. I could have because I'm a junkie and junkies are like crazy.

His mustache reminded me of Adolf Hitler`s styled mustache. He seemed like he had a bunch of carrots up his behind.

Our hands shook as I gently squeezed his hand. I could feel the warm grip of Mr. Swansinner`s hand. He tried to intimidate me with his tight grip, but I felt nothing. Bellduh watched as her father and I shared a stare down contest. His eyes had burned a hole into my own eyes. He had felt how cold my hand was as I gripped his.

"Edworth, you have a really cold hand. It doesn`t seem that cold outside today. Bellduh has told me so much about you."

"It`s always a pleasure, Sir. Bellduh has told me so much about you as well. So I hear you like dogs, cats, and squirrels."

Gees, I couldn't believe I said that. I was actually embarrassed that those words came out of my mouth. I would have said anything since I was so nervous. Bellduh looked embarrassed for me, and Mr. Swansinner giggled. That was just one step closer to Bellduh`s sweet blood.

"Well, Edworth, I`m glad that you think I like dogs, cats, and squirrels. I also like hurting things. Did you know that? Did Bellduh tell you what a great fighter I am? That`s right, I like to hurt animals and people. It`s my hobby. I shoot and hurt them when I`m out hunting. Doesn`t matter what animal I hurt, as long as I hurt one. Scared yet?"

"My dad was like so joking! Don`t worry about it, Edworth. Dad, you were just joking as always."

"That`s right, Edworth. I was just pulling your arm out of your socket. I`m a joker, one big joker."

"I knew that. This is a peaceful town. I didn`t believe it for a second."

"Sure, Edworth. I believe you, son. You were just ready to fly out my front door."

"Mr. Swansinner, you are right. I was getting ready to crash out the front door. You got me good. You're good, you. You're so funny, Mr. Swannsinner."

"What do you mean, Edworth? How am I funny? Do you think I'm a big joke? Tell me, Edworth. How am I funny? Funny in what way?

"I... it was a joke," I said.

"So… Edworth, what are your gruesome plans for my daughter? Now don`t be lying to me now. I want the truth, only the truth, and nothing but the truth."

"Dad, Edworth only wants what's best for me."

"No, no, Bellduh. It`s ok; I can speak for myself. The truth is, I really would like your permission to see more of Bellduh, Sir. The truth is; I`m a junkie. I want to tasteBellduh`s red honey and suck her dry. Bellduh`s red rum smells so good; I can`t help myself, Sir. I wanted to taste every student in the classroom at school, to impress Bellduh, but I didn`t. That`s how disciplined I am. You can trust me with your daughter Bellduh, Sir. I know I`m a junkie, but just give me a chance to prove myself, and you will see that I am not a bad junkie. I wouldn't mind tasting your red wine, Sir."

"Oh no, you didn`t! Edworth, I can`t believe you just told my father the truth!"

"Yes, yes I did. Trust me Bellduh. Honestly, it is the best policy."

Mr. Swansinner started laughing out loud.

"Edworth! You are seriously the man! I haven`t laughed this hard since I was in high school! You and Bellduh really played a good joke on me. Welcome to the family, Edworth. I look forward to more of your smart-ass jokes. That really made my day. Bellduh, don`t you dare let this one go, he is a keeper."

"Thanks. Whatever you say, I guess. Yes, Edworth and I really worked hard rehearsing that joke."

"Mr. Swansinner, I`m glad you loved the joke. Bellduh and I plan to get you again with another one sometime. You are an easy man to please, Mr. Swansinner. I`m really happy that you have welcomed me into the family. I am very happy to be seeing your daughter, Bellduh. She can have such an attitude sometimes, but since she is your daughter, I will be easy on her."

"Edworth, Son, don`t ever let Bellduh give you attitude. I know how she can be hard. You just take charge and show her who`s boss. You will have good moments and bad moments, but I`m sure you will overcome them. Just take it one day at a time, Edworth."

"Sweet deal, Mr. Swansinner. I will take your advice and do whatever it takes to make sure things go well between Bellduh and I. Relationships are never easy."

"No, you are right about that, Edworth. I know a thing or two about relationships. Marriage can be a real bitch."

Act 9

Every single day at Eclipse High was like a soap opera. You loved one day and despised another. Everyone gazed at me from the other end of the hallway as I walked in Bellduh's direction. She looked at me as if she wanted to tell me something.

She was not smiling and had a tense look on her face. That made me nervous, as I admired her beautiful complexion. There was no time to check my hair and do my makeup. Bellduh should have done me a favor and kept far away from me. I was not prepared to be cornered by her or her beautiful stench of blood.

I seriously did not want to confront Bellduh since I felt like I was having such a bad hair day. My breath smelled like my last bloody meal, and I could have just gone insane! I needed some breath mints fast. I needed to get a hold of myself. How could this have been happening to me? I wondered if I was having a Bellduh withdrawal.

I wanted Bellduh to stop looking at me since I felt that I looked like crap. I stuck my head in my locker, as if to reach for something. I hoped that it would distract her to move on, just that one time.

It was my best attempt at avoiding her. I prayed that it was going to work. I slowly peeked to see if Bellduh was still gracing me with her beautiful eyes. Bellduh caught my eyes in the act, and it was so awkward.

Bellduh was practically marching towards me, and I could smell her from where I was standing. Bellduh smelled so scrumptious. I wanted to drink her red liquor in front of everyone, but I knew that I could never show my perfect face again. I quickly inhaled to relish her scent. It just killed me to be in that situation. I just had to simply endure every second of it.

I absolutely hated school with a passion, but with Bellduh walking the halls of Eclipse High, I thought that I would stay a while. Bellduh made almost everything worthwhile. She was as sensational as they came.

We could have made love right then and there, but I was temporarily friendzoned by Bellduh. I wanted to grab her, and I wanted to kiss her. I was in love with her blood. Bellduh

40

was very beautiful, and she made me this way. It was all Bellduh's fault. I couldn't help but feel that way.

I was sure that she had some sort of magical spell on me and all of the guys at Eclipse High. I wondered if that witchcraft she liked to practice took control of her life. Even the girls had girl crushes on Bellduh. I wondered how that was possible since Bellduh wasn't the best-looking girl around. It was like totally ridiculous. No girl should have been as hot smelling as Bellduh. It should have been illegal.

She was just too much for Eclipse High. Bellduh was like royalty. All she had to do was ask me to do anything for her, and I would have in a heartbeat.

Bellduh was the cause of my obsession. There was a possibility that she could have been the one for me. It didn't really matter to me if she wanted just to be friends, but I hoped it was not forever. Just friends simply sucked. I felt this strong connection with Bellduh's blood.

I undressed her with my eyes. She obviously didn't get much sun living in this crap town of Eclipse. The local weatherman practically forecasted cloudy days every week.

The odd day would be sunny out. I thought I was pale, but Bellduh was almost like a ghost. I was so pale that I lightly powdered my face with some blush. Bellduh had her moments of looking great. Bellduh just loved to wear nice miniskirts, and had nice smooth legs.

I couldn't help but admire myself. I loved to impress every girl since I had a reputation to maintain. I had to stuff my pants sometimes to make myself look well hung. The girls loved judging guys by the bulge in their tight blue jeans. I really stuffed my pants for all the attention. I added a touch of stuffing to make my butt look firmer since I had a flat butt.

My bulge looked very reassuring. Every guy at Eclipse High copied me with my tight blue jeans. I had started a really nice trend. I loved every single day of it, and I was a total sex symbol. I was pretty sure that Bellduh enjoyed seeing me all dolled up. Bellduh could have used a little lesson from me about how to apply makeup. I was that good.

I could honestly say that I enjoy a little mascara and a touch of red lipstick. I loved to wear a hint of pink blush on my high cheekbones. Even the girls at Eclipse High could not compete with the way I wore my makeup. I should have probably given them some tips.

I loved to wear heavy cologne. It still didn't mask Bellduh's breathtaking sweet smell of blood. I wanted to drink her right away. My dad was the town's dentist. That explained my perfectly—heavenly white teeth.

I had a smile that mesmerizes a crowd. I had the opportunity to make the cover of a magazine and every perfect guy should. I was the perfect junkie, yet I didn't really belong at Eclipse. I was way too good for the town. I admit that sometimes I used a little too much lipstick, but people still adored me.

If Bellduh only knew how much I loved her blood. I fantasized that her blood and I were together forever. I would fantasize that her blood would be in a glass container, and I would take a sniff of it while sitting by the fireplace. My ultimate fantasy is too strong for words. Her blood and I would never be apart. I loved my fantasies about Bellduh's blood.

I walked the hallway as if I walked a supermodel runway. I walked with my chin up; my feet were in the perfect walking position, and I looked ahead of the crowd, knowing that everyone was investing their attention to me only. I loved to smell the different scents of blood. I had this half smirk on my face that showed that I was pleased with all of the attention I was getting. I was so very conceited and proud of it.

The students stood aside and observed me as I walked down the hallway. I wanted someone to roll out the red carpet before I entered the school. They seemed to admire my every move. Students gathered as if they waited to receive an autograph or even the privilege of my eyes meeting their own eyes. I was a total superstar at Eclipse High. You didn't dare talk to me unless I spoke to you. One girl tried to talk to me, but it was like a total fail. She went right up to me, to make small talk. As she spoke to me, she had this kind of spell on her, which made her mumble her words.

She was so embarrassed that she ran away from me and was laughed at by all the students at Eclipse High. She was totally humiliated, but I had a lot of respect for that poor girl. She had the courage to talk to me, and at least she did what no girl at Eclipse High dared to do.

I could have scarred you for life at Eclipse High if you couldn't successfully talk to me. The girls of Eclipse High all had their mouths dropped like a bunch of dogs as I walked by them.

One word from my beautiful mouth and any girl would listen, and she would have obeyed my every command. I didn't blame them. I bet that I could have put them all on a leash and taken them out if I really wanted to. I would have done anything Bellduh wanted at her command. I would have been her slave. I would have let her put me on a dog leash if that meant I could have her blood.

She never caught me off guard, since I could smell her beautiful erotic blood, as soon as she was close by.

Bellduh pretended not to notice me as I stood by my locker. She made her way behind me, and I felt her heart beating a million beats a second. I wondered what she wanted. I felt like I was being stalked, and I kind of felt violated.

"Hello, Edworth Cuddles."

She spoke. Bellduh had just spoken to me. I needed to do something fast. It was only Bellduh; she was only the girl with the blood of my dreams. I only fantasized about her blood every second. Her blood was so hot. Her blood was like the hottest at Eclipse High. Bellduh was a girl with truly the most beautiful red rum that I had ever smelled.

I was Edworth Cuddles, so there was no need to be shy. I was perfection, and it was impossible to top me. My eyes were intimidating, and my hair was lethal to the naked eye. A quick touch of my hair was extremely mesmerizing. One look into my eyes and your eyes would burn with passion. I slowly turned around to face Bellduh. I had never been so aroused in my life. I didn't know what to say yet. I was totally frozen with lust for Bellduh's blood.

She stared right into my eyes. Her eyes were dreamy, and they seemed to hypnotize me for a moment. I wondered if she wanted me right then and there.

I would have done anything for her blood. All she had to do was ask me, and I would have been her slave for life. I needed a sample of her blood and fast.

"Hello, uh, Bellduh," I murmured.

"We seriously need to talk in private, Edworth Cuddles. We really have to settle things and just sort things out. I can't explain it right now. Edworth, you and I need to meet up somewhere and discuss this thing," she demanded.

My mouth dropped, and I was like so excited to discuss things with Bellduh.

Bellduh moved her face close to my ear, and she whispered something in my ear. Her breath was warm and really made me quiver with lust. She let out sprinkles of her saliva on the side of my face while she whispered. I loved her bloody scent, but she needed to say it, not spray it.

Every girl around us was fascinated with Bellduh's sudden move to talk to me. They immediately started gossiping. It only took a few seconds for the whole town of Eclipse to get updated, when it came to news about us, Edworth Cuddles and Bellduh Swansinner. I wondered if it was also going to be on the local news. She was being very mysterious. That was beautiful to me. Almost everything Bellduh did was arousing to me.

She finished giving me the precious details of where and when to meet up with her. That moment with Bellduh felt like an eternity. I couldn't believe that it happened to me. It felt like a dream. I could feel the burning tension between us. Bellduh slowly looked away from me and walked away as she took her blood with her.

I took advantage of the moment. I took a huge sniff of Bellduh's beautiful smelling blood as she walked away from me. I didn't want her to leave, but it was meant to be.

I wanted things to go down differently. Everyone followed Bellduh and observed me. I know they wanted to ask what Bellduh wanted with me. I was suddenly a household name. People loved rumors, rumors, and more rumors. I didn't tell them anything since they didn't dare to approach me. Only a select few didn't care to approach me. I wouldn't have given them any of the juicy details even if they had asked me. I wanted to keep those details to myself.

I didn't think that Bellduh would have wanted me to tell people anything. Some things should have been kept secret, and everyone should have just minded their own business, but they were like a mob and didn't care about other people's privacy. I wished that I had just sucked the blood out of Bellduh and showed everyone my true unexpected nature. I could have definitely used a light taste of her scrumptious blood in my mouth. All I wanted was a little sample of her blood. I wondered if I was wanting too much too soon. I needed to know what it tasted like. It killed me inside and out. It killed me right, left, north, south, east, and west.

I was back to my usual routine of going to classes and going home. Bellduh's blood was all that I thought about.

The days had passed the same way as I wondered about Bellduh. I had planned to take Bellduh out on a date. I was very hopeful about it. She was just one big mystery.

I wanted to try to tell Bellduh how important a good education was to me in order to impress her. I figured that was lame, but I had to try something. I was hot, and I knew it. I was better than everyone, and I knew it. I could only dream of touching Bellduh's blood.

Act 10

Eclipse High school was such a drag. I walked into the cafeteria, and I tried to fit in since I felt like I didn't belong there. The first person I noticed was Bellduh, who looked much hotter that day than usual. I wondered what her plans were for the day.

Well, one thing was for sure, her blood was dreamy. Her blood was just perfect. Bellduh's blood was perfect, perfect, perfect! Bellduh was arguing with Jacub Blacky. There was something that some people didn't know about Bellduh. She could be a real drag sometimes. Jacub Blacky was the weirdest kid in Eclipse and an easy target.

That was an interesting day at school. Every single day in the life of Bellduh Swansinner was an unpredictable day. Everyone in the cafeteria just stopped what they were doing to watch the action.

First, let me remind you about Bellduh. I must defend her before I go on. She was the girl of my junkie dreams. I used to get so nervous when I was around her that I froze up. Every guy in school wanted her since she was the new girl, but I thought that maybe she had put a spell on everyone. I really wanted to hurt every guy in school, but I was a very nice junkie. Bellduh's blood drove me crazy inside.

I swear I could have drained her of her red stuff, but it was not right. Her blood smelled so respectable.

Some of the students were up to no good. Some came from poor families and loved to get as much money as they could from the weak. They bullied Jacub Blacky. They walked right up to Jacub Blacky and grabbed him. They pushed Jacub and backed him up to the wall.

Jacub Blacky was a total nerd and a wimp. He was really tanned, with ugly glasses, and I think he was like from Mexico or something. He was really smelly, and I could smell him from far, but Bellduh's blood did a fabulous job of overpowering the ugly stench. His hygiene was very bad. Jacub and his entire gang of friends had like this thick hairy unibrow. It was their signature or something.

"Hey stinky, did you bring my lunch money today?" Demanded the bully.

"Couldn't you call me Jacub?" Jacub pleaded.

"Stinky, were you born smelly or did you have to work on it?"

"Uh, like... a little of both? Is this like... a trick question?"

Everyone in the cafeteria cracked up, and I tried to hold in my laughter, but it was too much to handle. I covered my mouth as I let out my laugh.

Apparently, Jacub's kind does not allow him to wear deodorant. He is part of this animal pack or something. They have this thing for animal rights, especially for dogs.

To be honest, Jacub looked like a dog, but an ugly dog. He was not attractive at all. Any girl would have to be paid like millions of dollars to date Jacub.

"I...I got your lunch money today. No worries... Here is all ten bucks of it."

Jacub's friends did not even stick up for him. They were hiding in a corner like a bunch of scared puppies. That was really nice of them. What kind of friends don't help another friend out? Bellduh and her weird friends were sitting down and laughing as Jacub got bullied. The bully bitch-slapped Jacub!

"Wedgie time!" The bully shouted.

The bully had put Jacub on the floor and gave him a wedgie. I think Jacub actually let the bully do what she wanted with him for obvious reasons. Jacub was such a pervert. Some of the teachers were watching the action, and they did nothing to stop it since they must have been under Bellduh's spell. She finally tore out Jacub's underwear as everyone died of laughter. The bully took a sniff of his underwear and was disgusted. She threw Jacub's underwear into the crowd of onlookers. Everyone ran for their lives, and I didn't blame them. No one wanted Jacub's filth on them. That could have tainted them for life.

"Come on! That was like my favorite pair of underwear!" Jacub shouted.

The bully let out her crazy machine gun laugh. It was a very obnoxious laugh.

"Don't make me ask you for the money again, Stinky! I saw you try to sneak by me, but I could smell you coming my way Stinky! Let me give you some advice. Take a shower!" The bully shouted.

"I can shower, but only once a week to conserve water. I'm all for the environment. You should think about going green. My kind doesn't believe in masking our real scent."

The bully let out a machine gun laugh as her weird friends laughed along with her.

"Don't forget about my homework. You were late the last time, Stinky. You wouldn't want me to fail Spanish class now would you, Stinky? I didn't think so."

The bully grabbed the money from Jacub and let him go.

I couldn't take it anymore. I rushed up to Jacub and his pack of smelly friends. They saw me coming closer to them. They all shouted out my name with smiles. "Edworth!"

As soon as I got closer, their nasty stench had gotten worse. I placed my hand on my nose for at least some cover. Yep! It was bad! It really, really stunk. It was absolutely disgusting. It smelled like garbage, onion burgers, beer, popcorn, piss, and puke.

"Oh, come on Edworth, put your hand down. We don't smell that bad," Embrioze said.

Embrioze was very smelly. Some people called them the puppy pack. There were all kinds of names for these guys at Eclipse High. They tried too hard to fit in. They were a pathetic pack. Embrioze was sitting with Fared, Raul, and Tule, who were pretty much all alike. All of them were pretty smelly, but Jacub was seriously the Alpha and the most disgusting of the pack.

"Honestly, I don't smell anything. I have this cold, and it is like really runny today. Jacub, you seriously need to stop giving that bully your milk money. You seriously need to stop. It bugs me to see you get pushed around like that, Stinky… I mean, Jacub."

Jacub looked at me with sad puppy eyes.

"I am not the fighting type of guy, Edworth. How could I ever hurt someone, especially someone as beautiful as that bully? She is pretty hot for a bully."

"Jacub Blacky, do you have a crush on that bully?" I asked

The pack laughed at Jacub.

"Yes! Jacub has a little thing for the girl bully!" Embrioze shouted.

I tried not to laugh, but I just couldn't resist. I started to crack up! I just couldn't stop laughing.

"I do not! Stop it guys! Don't tease me!" Jacub shouted.

Jacub rushed out of the cafeteria in embarrassment.

I continued to laugh. How could someone be such a wimp? Jacub Blacky seriously needed to take some steroids or something.

I made my way to the food bar, though I didn't like to eat food. I walked over and pretended that I was getting food, just to fit in. I looked around, and I was disgusted with everything that I saw. Food was just so foul to me, and it really stunk too.

Too bad they didn't have Bellduh's blood on the menu. I started to pick out anything, just to make it look like I ate. I didn't want people to think that I had some sort of eating disorder.

I was rather impressed with the food display. They had practically everything. I saw shrimp, lobster, Chinese food, greasy fries, and other stuff. I thought about taking a banana. I thought that there was a chance that Bellduh loved bananas. I wanted to offer it to her. I took my time since I was in no rush to sit down with all that food.

I smelled something nasty. I thought it was rotten eggs and socks, but I didn't think that the school sold that there. I turned and attempted to grab the banana, which happened to be the last one there, yet it was a little wrinkly. I noticed Jacub was nearby, and he smelled rotten, but Bellduh's blood slightly overpowered his stench.

Bellduh was suddenly beside me, and I grabbed the banana as I was distracted by Bellduh's blood. Suddenly, I carelessly dropped the banana and everything suddenly moved in slow motion. I watched as the banana made its way to the dirty floor. I was so distracted that the banana hit the floor. I picked it up from the dirty floor.

"Bellduh, it looks like this banana almost got away. It's the last one, and I thought you might want it," I said.

"You've just like dropped your banana. It just like fell on the floor, Edworth. Isn't there like a two-second rule for food that drops on the floor?" Bellduh asked.

"Well, I think it was only like a second and a half. I actually counted. You can have the banana. I was actually saving it for you."

"It looks kind of mashed up and beaten, Edworth. You can keep your banana, but thanks.

"It's not so bad, Bellduh. I'm sure you can make like banana muffins with it. I know it looks pretty mashed up, but I hear bananas taste better that way."

"I suppose I could take it home and make banana muffins, Edworth. You're very thoughtful, thanks."

"I knew you would like the banana, Bellduh. You just seem like the banana type of girl."

I couldn't believe I said that. I was a little embarrassed, but Bellduh's blood was getting to me.

"Edworth, come hang out with me for lunch if you like."

"I would love that thanks, Bellduh."

We walked over to meet up with some of Bellduh's so-called friends. Rebecca saw me coming. Rebecca had an annoying laugh. Rebecca was such a bimbo, with pigtails and braces. She was always so happy. She called Bellduh by her first and last name as if they had just met, which was very unusual.

"Bellduh Swansinner, we meet again! Guess what I just heard?" Rebecca said.

I was not a fan of Rebecca. I wanted to suck her blood and then slap her. She was so irritating, but she made me laugh sometimes. I always wanted to taste Rebecca, but I was taught to stay polite and greet everyone as a friend. Yes, this is my life. I'm Edworth Cuddles, the friendly junkie.

"Um... Rebecca, this is Edworth Cuddles," Bellduh said.

"Edworth! So nice to meet you, finally. I heard so much about you!"

"Pleasure to meet you," I said.

"So like... guess who Casper is dating right now? OMG, Bellduh! You are so not going to believe who Casper is dating! I will give you a clue..." Rebecca babbled.

Wow, just wow. Rebecca talked about my family in front of me, no shame.

As Rebecca babbled on about Casper, I could tell you the last person Casper dated was Kermit Cuddles. Kermit was related to me, sort of. Casper was part of the family, but he was adopted, it's a long story. Dating each other was acceptable in my family circle.

"Just tell me already, please!" Bellduh begged.

Rebecca smiled and giggled.

"Casper is dating the one and only... Roosilly! Can you believe it?"

"I'm shocked. I really didn't see that coming," Bellduh said.

"Like, it's so unreal, right? How can Casper go from Kermit to Roosilly? I really thought Casper and Kermit would get back together," Rebecca babbled.

"Life works in mysterious ways. Roosilly is one lucky girl," I said.

"Casper and Kermit are like never ever, ever, ever getting back together," Rebecca babbled.

The truth about my family was a little crazy. There were things about Casper and Kermit that people didn't know. They used to be tight lovers. They would make love in the boy's washroom and even smoke weed.

I heard some other stories about them. They were the queerest couple apparently. There was no stopping them at parties.

They were the life of the party. If they weren't together, people would think something was wrong, and rumors would spread around school like wildfire. Apparently, Roosilly had this big crush on Casper for a while, and it turned out that Casper swung both ways. No one had a clue that Casper would ever swing the other way. It was as if Casper was turning to the dark side by being with Roosilly.

"Speak of the devil. Look who just walked in," Rebecca babbled.

We turned our heads to discover that the rumors were true.

Casper and Roosilly walked into the cafeteria, hand in hand. It was as if they were approaching an altar, to be married. Roosilly was looking like the bitch that she was, and made all the other girls jealous.

Casper was looking rather silly. He had his dyed black hair slicked back like a model, with his big green eyes, plump lips, high cheekbones, and broad shoulders. He wore a little makeup as well. That seemed like the in thing to do at Eclipse High. Casper and Roosilly walked like slow motion, as everyone watched the couple in envy. It seemed like there was wind blowing at them, blowing smoothly through Roosilly's lovely hair, which was not better than my hair.

Casper had a bad history of blood sucking. He wanted to suck everyone dry.

Nothing was as pleasing as the scent of Bellduh's blood.

The class was about to start. It was time for music class. This was definitely one of the best classes in school, since Bellduh was in my class. The first few classes she sat in the back of the class, where all the weird people sat. I made my way to class and took my seat.

The teacher assigned seats, which Bellduh happened to take a seat next to me. I couldn't believe how lucky I was. Everyone prepared for music class and tried out their musical instruments.

Bellduh looked at me, and she gave me a strange look. I smiled at her. I could smell her, and her blood smelled so worthy. If only she could have read my mind.

I took a deep breath, and I was amazed at how great Bellduh's blood smelled during music class. The music must have triggered something in Bellduh. I was actually tempted to rip up the class and suck the blood right out of Bellduh's smooth neck. Bellduh glanced at me and smiled.

She couldn't get enough of my perfectly feathered hair, my unusual eyes, perfectly white teeth, and my beautiful red lips that were to die for. My eyebrows were perfectly shaped. She loved the way I held my violin, but then again, who didn't?

I really wanted Bellduh's blood with a passion. I could have made out with her on the floor, and in front of the class. The class was really pathetic. Not one person knew how to play the violin, except for Bellduh and myself. We were more than decent. We seemed to have a natural talent for playing the violin.

The music teacher, Miss Hanna, who had attractive smelling blood, asked me to play the violin in front of the class. I absolutely loved Miss Hanna for asking me. She looked at me as if she wanted to have a romantic encounter with me. I could have just imagined Miss Hanna and I together.

I would have probably met up with Miss Hanna after class, and I would have probably tried to get anything I could get from her. There was nothing like free blood. I would have loved to have Miss Hanna on my dinner table in a nice tall glass. Anyone that looked at me the way Miss Hanna did was asking for their blood to get sucked out by me.

At least it did not really happen. My imagination had run wild again. I knew how to really influence the opposite sex. I seemed to have this power over girls. It must have been a nature talent of mine.

I agreed to demonstrate my musical talent. I was about to play my violin in front of the class. I looked forward to this with a passion.

I cleared my throat, and Bellduh happened to glance at me.

My mouth happened to drop as she glanced at me. I could hear her heart beating really fast. I was like a statue standing above the class, and I was perfect.

I took a deep breath as I prepared to play my violin. The room was completely silent as all the girls, and even the boys looked forward to watching me play my violin.

The teacher looked aroused. I really wanted to suck her blood right out of her body. I started to play my violin.

I played my violin so sweetly and romantically. Bellduh had never seen that side of me before. I learned something new every class. This seemed very romantic, and there was a lot of passion.

I never thought that I would ever see that day. I felt the passion flow through my body. I could feel the high temperature of Bellduh's blood surge through me as I played.

Bellduh closed her eyes as I played my violin. She occasionally opened her beautiful eyes, to randomly glance around the classroom. She glanced at me, and she pauses for a few seconds.

I was frozen as I stared deeply into her eyes. I thought that one second felt like an eternity.

Bellduh slowly glanced away and closed her eyes as I continued to play my violin. The room was relaxing, romantic, and hot. I felt the tension in the room. I could smell Bellduh's blood, overpowering everyone else's.

I finished my romantic music, and the class applauded. Bellduh smiled, and I took my seat.

"I never knew you had it in you, Edworth," Bellduh said.

I looked directly into Bellduh's eyes.

"Don't forget about our little get together," I said.

She was captivated by my stare.

"I wouldn't miss it for the world," she said.

Bellduh stared at me and smiled. Her glowing white teeth brighten up the room.

"Let me ask you something Edworth. Why are you so romantic?" she asked.

I was speechless. Bellduh actually noticed. I wondered if she was truly in love with me. There was only one way to find out.

"When we have that meeting, maybe I will give you a straight answer, Bellduh."

Bellduh looked at me with a smile, and we carried on with our music class. It felt so magical. Anyone would have paid to experience that priceless moment.

Bellduh looked forward to many more classes of me playing my violin. I played as if nobody was watching. I played my violin with passion and took my violin very seriously.

I adored every second of it. We continued to practice our music. Bellduh was very talented for a witch. I wondered what other talents she had. I was going to find out one of these days. Bellduh was not perfect, but her blood was flawless. Bellduh wanted more and more of my lovely music. She couldn't get enough of it. I knew how to play my violin with a passion.

Act 11

Everything had gone downhill when my family and I moved to the lousy town of Eclipse. My family and I were probably the only nice junkies in Eclipse, and it had gotten very lonely at times. I used to wonder if there were others like us, and then I found out there were. If there were any others, we hadn't seen them. We had hoped to find more of our kind. Hopefully, they were nice junkies. It would have felt more comfortable. I would not have felt so out of place. They would have had to be as friendly as me.

I just didn't seem to fit in. I used to pretend that everything was fine, but they knew that I didn't belong in Eclipse. I had thought about joining a freak show, but that didn't exactly work.

I hunted for blood most of the time. I lived off mostly animals. My dad and I had evolved. We tried to be normal. My dad was very fond of hunting on his spare time. He had a lot of spare time. He wouldn't stay home and play video games all day.

Let's just say that he and I never went hungry. We had a nice blood supply in our home. Going hungry was not a nice feeling. Our cabinets were filled with a large blood supply. Animal blood mostly. There was other blood, but mostly from bad people, trust me. If my dad had used an innocent person's blood, he might have kept that to himself. He had gotten greedy from time to time since any blood from a person was priceless.

When I arrived home, I had thought of Bellduh and wondered what she is up to. I never had anything better to do, yet I enjoyed thinking of Bellduh. My dad was never home, just me. The other members of my family had their own places and came as they pleased.

Sometimes, I loved just watching vampire movies after school, and kicking back sipping on a bottle of blood. Life wasn't always this peaceful. This is one of the reasons my family and I moved to Eclipse.

My dad walked into the living room from a long day of hunting. He had his green camouflage outfit on, as if he really needed it.

"I see you're having a bloody cold one, Edworth. How was school today? Did you make any friends today?"

I hated it when my dad asked me questions like that. He always asked the same thing every day. It made me feel like such a child. My dad could be such a nag. How could I have possibly made friends, when all I wanted to do was drink them? I couldn't even have a girlfriend with my cravings.

"Call me lazy, dad. All I want to do is nothing, just relax and drink blood. I'm not a child, remember? School was just the usual, just wanted to taste everyone in my path. Catch anything big today?"

My dad showed me a bottle of blood and he smiled. I thought that he was up to no good.

"See this Edworth; it's the blood of a handsome young lad who seemed to think that I was an animal. I will be drinking hard tonight!"

My dad had actually drained a bad person. He must have been aggravated to practically milk the poor guy. I thought my dad was a liar. He just missed blood from a person too much. This was just horrible. I had to act like it meant nothing to me. I hated when the junkie policy was broken because it was not who we were. We were nice junkies, most of the time.

"I think I will join you tonight," I said.

"Sounds like a plan. I want to see you with some friends over so go out, and get a girlfriend. You should socialize. Be normal, Edworth. Be normal for a day."

I smiled at my dad as he sat beside me. I raised my bottle of blood.

"Cheers!" I said.

My dad raised his bottle of blood.

"Here's to us, Edworth. Cheers!"

We enjoyed our quiet night together and enjoyed a vampire movie.

The next day, I was at my locker getting ready for class.

Someone smelly was approaching, and I knew exactly who it was. It was Jacub since I could smell his stench from a mile away. It was not a nice thing to smell in the morning, unless you liked the stench of dirty socks and smelly cheese. I pretended not to see him and made myself look busy. He approached Bellduh, who was socializing with others. It looked like I was about to witness some cheesiness.

"Bellduh! How are you Bellduh? Jacub asked.

I turned around to see that Jacub had brought a banana for Bellduh. Bellduh smiled and thanked him. I wondered why Jacub would give Bellduh a banana.

"Jacub, you really shouldn't have," Bellduh said.

"No, Bellduh. You gave me this letter, and I will read it out loud to everyone."

Everyone had gathered in the hallway around us. This was so embarrassing, but not for me. I felt really sorry for Jacub. Jacub's friends stood near him, with people covering their noses cause they stunk like rotten potatoes and sour milk. Bellduh's friends stood across, with the rest of the students gathered around to see what Jacub had up his sleeve. Jacub began to speak.

"I have this letter that Bellduh wrote to me. I found it in my math textbook. I want to read what she wrote to me."

Jacub continued to read the letter:

"Dear Jacub,

I have been watching you from far, and I just have to let my feelings go and tell you that you are so brave and smart, and sexy. You may have a strong odor, but I find it very manly. You are the boy of my dreams, and I love the way you smell.

I hope that when you read this letter, you will man up and ask me out. I want you bad. Please be mine. Pretty, please...

Your Secret Lover,

Bellduh Swansinner. XOX."

"I will now read this poem I wrote for Bellduh," Jacub said.

Jacub continued to read a poem that he wrote for Bellduh:

"Dear Bellduh,

You are beautiful and dreamy,

I really would like to cream on you,

Some say you're a witch,

At least you're not a bitch,

I know you want me,

You can fall in love with me,

I need you Bellduh,

Please be mine.

Bellduh, will you be my girl?" Jacub said.

My mouth dropped. Everyone was silent in disbelief.

"Jacub, I... never wrote you any letter; I'm sorry; I don't know what to tell you," Bellduh said.

Jacub was stunned! He backed away from Bellduh.

"If you didn't write this letter, Bellduh, then who wrote it?"

"I DID!" The bully shouted.

Everyone cracked up hysterically as Bellduh laughed out loud. Jacub shook his head. Jacub looked at Bellduh and then looked at me as I giggled. Jacub ran away as everyone cracked up. Even Jacub's friends were cracking up.

"You got owned! Owned!" The bully shouted as Jacub ran away.

"Don't... tease me...!" Jacub shouted as he ran off in tears.

I walked up to Bellduh as she looked up at me, still cracking up. The show was over as people made their way to their classes.

"Tonight, I want to meet up tonight," I demand.

Bellduh smiled as she looked at me.

"You want to meet tonight, then fine, Edworth. Let's do this. We always have something to argue about. Meet me in the black forest around 6 p.m."

I looked at Bellduh, and we had a mutual agreement.

Bellduh smiled at me and walked away. That was intense. I felt like sucking the blood out of Bellduh right then and there. I smelled her blood, and it made me hot, as I stood in front of her. It was a sweet moment.

As classes went on, I saw Bellduh again, as she walked nearby. I was about to make my way to class, and I saw that Alicia had gotten right in Bellduh's face. She was one of the most bizarre students at school, well, a junkie girl that is. I approached them to get in on the conversation since there were a few minutes to spare.

"Bellduh! Bellduh! Caramella! How are you… today?" Alicia asked.

She hugged Bellduh suddenly. Bellduh smiled and giggled.

"Alicia… Well, you know I'm the usual… just like yesterday. Alicia you are so cold… as if you are like a junkie or something."

As Alicia mumbled on, I pretended to listen as she spoke, but I just looked on at Bellduh and wondered about her. I wondered why she smelled so good.

I should have taken the next step. I should have planned something for the weekend with Bellduh. I thought that maybe a dinner for three with my dad would have been nice. I thought about sweetening up her blood by offering her some ice cream first. I knew that I probably had to wine and dine her. I didn't think that I wanted to just taste her blood. I wanted her around for a while. I could have done a candle light dinner with red wine. I always tried to be a romantic junkie.

I hoped that Bellduh would eat all the sweets that she could eat to sweeten up that tempting blood of hers. She may have been allergic to something, but I hoped not. I could still smell how erotic her blood was. It smelled so divine.

She was purely dessert. I wanted to make my dad very happy. He had a fetish for young, fresh red pulp. He might have wanted to have a taste. It would have also given me a chance to prove myself as a junkie. I should have probably waited to see how things worked between Bellduh and I. I was getting really carried away with all of this.

There was nothing wrong with daydreaming. One has to dream. Alicia was still babbling on as I fantasized about sucking the life out of Bellduh. Alicia responded to Bellduh's comment about being cold as a junkie.

"Imagine that, eh… me, a junkie," Alicia giggled.

I also laughed with Alicia, yet it was a fake laugh.

"We should get together, Alicia. How about we get to know each other better this weekend?" Bellduh asked.

"Like… that sounds like a plan, Bellduh! This is like a great opportunity for us to really bond. Heck, why not have a slumber party this weekend?" Alicia asked.

"That sounds like a plan. How about Saturday night?" Bellduh asked.

Alicia looked like she had just won the lottery or something.

"Yes, yes, yes! I can't wait, Bellduh! So, I have like no idea where you live, so here is my number and you can text me your address. We can plan our night out."

Bellduh smiled back at Alicia, and she took her number.

"Well, see you soon Alicia, can't wait," Bellduh said.

I gave Alicia a dirty look as she smiled at me and knew exactly why I was disappointed with her. Alicia walked off to her class, and I was off to my Chemistry class.

I took my seat. Casper arrived and took a seat beside me. Bellduh arrived and took a seat behind me. She sat alone for a short time. I looked behind me, and she smiled. I could feel her power over me. Our whole class had to be paired up. I hoped that Bellduh sat beside me for the next time.

"Be careful Casper, this one is a junkie," Bellduh murmured.

Casper looked at me and looked back at Bellduh.

"Let's not be mean to Edworth now. Edworth seems to be different from the rest of us, but you're alright, Bellduh," Casper said.

The Chemistry teacher, Mr. Raviolli, who happened to be totally Italian, was late. Bellduh was wasting time socializing with Angelina, who had just sat next to her.

Angelina dressed like a girl who practiced witchcraft, if you can imagine that. She was one of Bellduh's weird friends, and I believed they all practiced witchcraft together. She had her hair dyed red, and I thought she was the least popular girl at school.

I heard that Angelina hypnotized guys so that they would date her. She came from a poor family and took advantage of guys that she had dated by taking all their wallets. Listening to her talk to Bellduh was very irritating. I could hear Bellduh giggling with Angelina.

I could smell Angelina's blood from where I am sitting. Angelina's hot lava smelled pretty nice, but not anywhere close to Bellduh. I would have still loved to suck Angelina's blood, but I couldn't. I could have probably followed her after school and waited until the timing was right, and drained her blood to the last drop, but I could only fantasize about it. I was a good junkie.

Casper was just minding his own business. I was looking at him as he was admiring how great Bellduh smelled. I gave him a dirty look, and he knew to quit it. He was very hungry. I feared for Bellduh's safety.

Casper turned to make conversation with Bellduh.

"You want to ask me, don't you?" Casper asked.

Bellduh hesitated and was even shocked that Casper was speaking to her. I always thought that Casper was too good for a lot of people, especially Bellduh.

"Um… Ask you what?" Bellduh asked.

Casper looked at Bellduh with a smile.

Bellduh was a little stunned, and a little nervous to what Casper was talking about.

"Bellduh, you want to know if it's true about me."

"I really don't know what you're talking about, Casper."

Obviously, Casper thought highly of himself.

"Well, if you should know, yes… it's true. I was in a mental hospital and was released many years ago, but that's not what I really want to tell you. The rumors are true about Kermit Cuddles and I. He cheated on me, and I didn't even cheat on him, it's true. You know he cheated on me many times. I don't know why I'm telling you all this. I guess since you are the new girl and all that you might be interested.

Only a certain few know. There is something about you, Bellduh. You seem different. Well, I broke up with Kermit after catching him in the act with another guy, at Edworth's party, but there is a lot more that caused the break-up. Everyone thought the break-up was mutual, but I ended it. You know Kermit still wants me back."

I was shocked that Casper was telling Bellduh his private biography. I wondered what it was about Bellduh that made him feels so comfortable.

Maybe it was her pale white skin or her innocent eyes. Maybe they just had a natural chemistry. Maybe it was her beautiful scent of blood. I wondered if he would have ever dated Bellduh. I would have never allowed it.

There were so many open relationships at Eclipse High. Kermit, Roosilly, and Casper had been swapping each other like there was no tomorrow. I was confused at who was dating who. I was certain that Kermit and Roosilly were currently dating. It was bad if Kermit was dating Roosilly. They were not exactly a match made in heaven. They were more like a match made in the fires of hell.

Roosilly practically thought she owned Kermit. I really thought about drinking people that I disliked. I was dying to drink Bellduh's blood, but I really didn't want to hurt her. She made me feel at home. She smelled delightful.

"You have really been through a lot, Casper. I hope things work out for you," Bellduh said.

The teacher, Mr. Raviolli, finally arrived to class.

"I'm late today, sorry," Mr. Raviolli said.

Everyone in the classroom cheered and applauded. Bellduh was staring at me as the class was being taught. Mr. Raviolli was playing some boring movie. Bellduh's smell was keeping me sane. I started to daydream…

The movie was still on, but Casper was gone. No other student was around. I looked back to see that Bellduh was the only one in the classroom.

She was staring at me as I looked back at her. She didn't smile. I got up and went to her from behind. I took my hands and ran them around her neck. I ran my fingers through her beautiful hair. Bellduh leaned back as our eyes met. I slowly made my way to kiss her. Our lips were about to touch…

"Edworth, Edworth, oh Edworth, are you alive?" Casper asked.

Casper woke me from my fantasy! The timing could not have been worse. I smiled. I had really drifted off for several seconds. I was so caught up in the moment that it had felt so real.

"Yep, I'm still here, Casper. It's a boring movie though, but thanks for asking."

Casper smiled and put his attention back to the movie. I looked back to see Bellduh, who was already glancing at me, as if she was having the same daydream as I was. I turned back to watch the movie, but could still feel Bellduh's eyes burning a hole in my back.

The experience was really intense. With Bellduh around, who was like an angel, what more could any junkie ask for?

The class finally ended, and the day dragged on. I made my way to my locker to put away my stuff. Everyone seemed to just scatter like a herd of cattle.

 Bellduh seemed to have disappeared from sight, but I didn't forget about our meeting in the dark forest. I made my way outside, and I started walking to meet up with Bellduh.

I saw her close by me and continued to walk.

As I walked, I could smell cow manure. I guess it was that time of the year where farmers did their thing. As I walked towards the dark forest, the smell seemed to be getting worse. I looked around me, and I saw that Jacub was running towards me. He had such a foul stench.

"Bellduh! Wait up!" Jacub shouted.

He totally ignored me to talk to Bellduh, as I witnessed the conversation.

Bellduh, being the nice girl that she was, waited for Jacub to catch up to her. The smell was unbearable. Bellduh smiled at me and talked to Jacub as I took my time.

"Jacub... what are you doing here? I thought you lived on the other side of town," Bellduh said.

Jacub confronted Bellduh. He had a bottle of beer. It suddenly started to rain. Jacub smelled heavily like he'd been smoking up! I was shocked! I didn't figure Jacub for the smoking weed type. I guess he was really bummed out. I stood with them and listened to their conversation.

"Bellduh, now hear me out, please. I want to tell you something. You are... Bellduh."

Jacub was obviously high and drunk out of his stinky mind.

"Jacub how much beer have you been drinking? And what is that? Is that weed I smell? Since when are you a cool... guy, Jacub? You don't have to be like Edworth, to get me to like you. Just be yourself, and we will see what happens."

"Please, Bellduh, and you too Edworth, don't tell anyone about this. It's against my family's regulations. Zero tolerance! If anyone finds out that I have been drinking and smoking up, I will get 20 lashes in the butt! Promise me you won't tell on me," Jacub pleaded.

"Relax, Jacub. I won't say a word to anyone. Your secret is safe with us. Now tell me something, Jacub, what are you doing here in this rain?" Bellduh asked.

"Let me sing to you please, you will be impressed with me Bellduh. I can't sing, but I will try. I thought of a nice song for you."

Jacub really wanted to sing his song of his to Bellduh. I had a feeling I was going to be like totally embarrassed for him. He started to sing to Bellduh...

"Bellduh, I was humiliated the other day,

I want you to know that I think of you every day,

And I'm not even gay, like some people say,

Not that there is anything wrong with that, but I'm not,

Bellduh, I know I may look like a dog, but I don't really know what to say,

At least I'm not a junkie like some..."

Jacub was a God-awful singer, and even if he weren't drunk and high, I could still tell he would have been just as horrible. His voice was in every direction, and his pitch was just crackling like a dead cat or something.

Jacub continued to sing…

"I know I can be such a wimp, I can be such a smelly chimp,

I'm not so bad for you, Bellduh, I can cook for you, and dress you, feed you, and wash you, and do whatever you want me to, Bellduh,

I know I don't have much class, but at least I don't take it in the behind, like some people we know,

Not… not that there is anything wrong with that, and I'm not even fat, please be mine forever, Bellduh."

"Jacub, please stop singing," Bellduh said.

Jacub continued…

"I'm a giver, not a taker, and I'm not a faker, Bellduh,

I may be a virgin, but I still like to imagine you, and I, Bellduh, eating some warm apple pie, by the sky, staring in your eyes, with all kinds of flies, smelling your hair dyes, and sitting by the skies,

Someday soon, we could be going to the moon and be eating cartoons, with some spoons, Bellduh,

Maybe someday I will decide to take a shower just for you, and even bath in roses, just for you, and I won't smell like poo, cause I will use a lot of shampoo, just for you,

Do you like puppies that stink? I hope you do, Bellduh, cause I could be a puppy too, if I wanted me too, just for you,

The only one thing I would do, is you, Bellduh,

Unless you don't want me to,

I have a funny feeling about us Bellduh; it tickles, I feel giddy and hippy,

I feel pissy and a little sissy for you, Bellduh,

When I take a piss or dump, I want to hiss and get on you, and hump you too,

I know myself… I know I am not… I know I just am not good enough for someone like you… Bellduh…

Bellduh I may not smell like Edworth, but I am warmer than him,

I may not smell like roses Bellduh, but I will be yours,

Roses are red; violets are blue, you can call me Moses, and I will call you Sue, if you want me to,

Someday Bellduh, you will look at me and pee, and see the tree,

Bellduh there is something about me, you don't know Bellduh,

I'm sorry… I'm not man enough to tell you, Bellduh,

I don't even care that you're a witch, if you are; I won't bitch, Bellduh,

Someday Bellduh, I will… I will tell you about myself,

Things you don't know, Bellduh,

I have more to offer you than my smell, Bellduh,

I… I… gotta go Bellduh!"

Jacub finally finished singing, and Jacub ran away from us, crying! My mouth dropped. I was giggling, and then I was laughing in the rain and so was Bellduh. Jacub looked back in disgust.

He continued to run away crying. How could someone be such a baby? That was seriously pathetic. Jacub was the saddest boy in Eclipse. He needed a girlfriend badly.

What a sad little pup Jacub was. Gees! His singing stunk as bad as he did. He really put a lot of work into his song, but I could only tell the truth. He was pretty stoned. He really was a mystery.

I wouldn't have wanted anyone else to hear Jacub sing. It was like poison to my ears. I wouldn't have wanted people to have nightmares about him singing. It was bad enough that people at Eclipse had to smell his nasty stink. Well, no one was perfect, except for me, of course, and that's the way it was at Eclipse.

Bellduh and I looked forward to our meeting in the dark forest. I was pretty thirsty, and my dad didn't always bring home the freshest blood all the time. I told Bellduh to follow me and that I would show her about my true self.

We were now on our way into the forest to catch an animal. The forest was very quiet. I could usually hear the animals running around left and right, north and south. It was kind of slow in the forest with no animals running around.

The question was, what was I in the mood for? Maybe a bear, though I have never seen many bears around there, and my dad had claimed such kills. I could have sucked on a bunch of squirrels, rabbits, or maybe a bad person if I were lucky. I knew that I shouldn't taste people. I could never do that around Bellduh.

I was trying to be just like them. I needed to fit in around Eclipse.

It looked like a storm was coming, but I wasn't afraid to get wet. I wondered what Bellduh's plans were for that night. I was tempted to taste her since she smelled so good.

I wouldn't have shared Bellduh's blood with my dad. Her blood would have been too good to share with any junkie.

I heard a noise coming from across Bellduh and I. I could smell that it was not an animal. It was an unusual person. We should have probably kept moving since I didn't want any trouble.

I think I was born for trouble. Whoever it was had a very sweet-smelling blood. My natural instinct had taken over.

As we had gotten closer to the smell of blood, my mouth watered.

The strange person was nearby. We turned the corner of a tree, and we saw a young teenage girl. She looked at us and was startled. I couldn't seem to tell what she wanted. Bellduh took over and made conversation with the lost girl in the forest as I looked on.

"Where did you come from? You startled us," Bellduh asked.

The young girl looked at us with caution.

"I was just on my way out, heading home."

She was not a good liar. Something was up with this girl in the forest.

"Nothing like roaming the forest after school, eh? Looks like a storm is coming. I'm Bellduh, by the way, Bellduh Swansinner. This is Edworth Cuddles."

Bellduh offered her hand to shake hers, and the girl hesitated. She had finally decided to shake our hands. She looked like she felt better after shaking our hands. She looked at me funny, since my hand was so cold.

"I'm kinda hungry, just wondering where the closest place to eat is."

I decide to speak up.

"The closest place would probably be my place with my dad. It's not far from here. If you're hungry you can grab a bite to eat, I mean, if you want, like… we don't even know each other. Heck, what is your name anyway?" I asked.

The girl gave me a little smirk.

"I'm Brie Tanners. It's very nice to meet the both of you."

Bellduh smiled at Brie.

"Well, I guess you are a long way from home, Brie Tanners," Bellduh said.

Brie gave us a much bigger smile. She didn't dress well. Brie Tanners looked homeless. I thought that I should have offered her some cheese. She just might have been a cheap girl. All I was thinking about was ripping into her neck and feasting on her sweet blood.

I really wanted to bring Brie back home and drink her to the last drop. I also wanted my dad to see her. I wanted him to see what a good junkie I've been. I knew I would have made him proud.

"So... Where to now?" Brie asked.

"Follow Bellduh and I. I have a lot of cheese at my place. You must like cheese. It's not too far from here. You are going to love my place. It's pretty comfortable and warm. My dad would love to meet you," I said.

Brie hesitated.

"Oh. I… I'm not sure it's a good idea then. He might think I'm a delinquent."

Brie was really nervous about going to my place for food since I had mentioned my dad. Nevertheless, I had a feeling that she would give in.

Just by the smell of her blood, I could tell she hadn't eaten for hours, and she must have hungry and thirsty. I could tell that she loved cheese. My Dad would have had the opportunity to meet Brie.

"My dad would love to meet you, Brie! I will tell him you and I are friends from school. He will love your company, seriously. Why not sleepover too. I mean, if you like. You are welcome in my home anytime. I hope you, Bellduh, and I can get to know each other, and I will help you out anyway that I can. I know you must be hungry right now. You must want cheese, Brie. I'm hungry too. I say we all go and have a nice hot meal and sit back and watch a vampire movie."

"Thank you so much, Edworth. I really can't believe how kind you are. I guess it's no surprise that I love cheese. You don't know how much this means to me. I've been on my own for some time now. The truth is; I am starving. Where do we go from here?" Brie asked.

"No, it's no trouble. Bellduh and I both knew as soon as we saw you around here that you were away from home. This isn't exactly the place to hang out by yourself. There is no cheese in this forest. We should get going now. My home is not too far away."

Brie smiled, and we made our way through the dark forest. She was quiet. She actually helped take my mind off Bellduh. She followed us like a lost puppy.

She couldn't resist. I offered her cheese and shelter. Most of all, I offered my companionship. What lonely girl in a dark forest wouldn't want all of those things, especially cheese?

The storm was about to hit hard. We walked a little faster as the thunder erupted. After walking for a while, the lightning struck, and the rain came down hard. We finally reached my home, and I opened the door.

My home was not much. It was actually an abandoned cabin in the woods. However, my dad renovated the place. It may have looked like a little crappy from the outside, but it was fresh on the inside. My family was never home. It was always just me here.

My home was nice. It's all alone in the dark forest, but peaceful. I was proud of my home. As we walked inside, I noticed Brie could not believe her eyes at how beautiful my place was.

She took the time to admire the art on the walls and glanced over at the fireplace. The fire had been burning night and day. In fact, we never put out the fire.

The fire represented life and my dad, and I loved to sit around the fireplace. I loved to sit around, and read a good book around the fireplace, where it was nice and peaceful.

"Make yourself at home Bellduh, and you too Brie. What's mine is yours."

Bellduh didn't say much. She concentrated on Brie.

Brie looked at me and glanced around with a smile.

"Edworth, this is such a beautiful home you have. How long have you been living here?" Brie asked.

"My family and I have not been here long. We actually just started renovating the place, and I'm known as the know it all around here. I haven't really had much help. More like no help since I'm the only one in my family that is handy."

"This sure beats any place that I have ever lived in. I don't have a lot of money, and I move from place to place. I couldn't afford much cheese. You have it really nice here, Edworth. You are lucky to have such a good life here," Brie said.

"Thanks for saying such nice things. There is a lot more to me than you know."

We all sat down on the couch by the fire, and we talked. We talked a lot about cheese. I tried to keep Brie occupied as long as I could until my dad arrived home. I got Brie and Bellduh a glass of water and some cheese and crackers.

I let them know that dinner would start when my dad arrived. Brie devoured the food, finished the water, and caught her breath. She thanked me and started to make some interesting conversation.

She talked about how she was living with an abusive boyfriend who always wanted her to feed him slices of cheese. It was some sort of fetish of his. She dropped out of school and had been on her own for a while. She would steal cheese from the store. She managed to

70

make her way into the dark forest. She loved grilled cheese sandwiches. Her parents used to own a cheese factory until the mice took over, and they went bankrupt.

After a long walk, she lost her way and was lost. She didn't know if she would have found her way out if it weren't for me. She didn't know if she would ever eat cheese again.

I told her my story and about all the crazies at school. I mentioned Bellduh to her and how in love I was with her. Brie was very fascinated with hearing about Bellduh and myself.

Bellduh was nothing but smiles, hearing me say such things.

Brie told us about her abusive relationship. Her boyfriend would hurt her mentally and physically. He would also steal her cheese that she had stolen. Her boyfriend would call her fat and told her to lose weight.

Brie was to the point that she was so mentally abused, and she had become anorexic. Her serious eating disorder almost killed her. She was lucky, and she eventually started to eat again, mostly cheese.

She never wanted to be called fat ever again. She would rather have been called skinny than to have someone call her fat.

He would push her and hit her when he would get drunk and punch her in the face. He forced cheese slices down her throat. She would get daily whippings by him and his friends. She did dirty favors for money so that she could buy cheese.

Brie turned to alcohol. She would shoplift anything and anywhere. She was a good shoplifter. After everything she had been through, she never got caught shoplifting. She was very sneaky and fast, like a ninja. Things had gotten very bad very fast for her.

She was desperate. Her abusive boyfriend came home one night and was so high on crack that he would beat her and beat her with his belt. He would pull her hair, take his pocket knife, and poke her body with it.

He would take his cigarettes, lighter, and burn her butt and legs. She stayed with him cause she had nowhere else to go. She was scared and dependent on him for shelter, and everything else that was a necessity, especially cheese.

One night he threatened to take away her cheese, so that was the night she had run away. Her mom went missing, and her dad was into drugs and got blown up while he was in his truck.

She had no other family. Her life was ending faster and faster. I wondered if she wanted to eat more cheese. I wanted to put her out of her misery, but I couldn't.

Maybe this is why we crossed paths. Bellduh and I listened to her sad little story, and I felt really bad for her. I was still hungry though. Brie continued to tell us what she liked to do in her spare time. She loved to read, loved animals, and especially loved to eat cheese. She wished she had a puppy. She's always been poor, most of her life, and did not have the luxury of such things.

"I'm so sorry to hear that, Brie. That's very sad news. I hope things will get better from here," Bellduh said.

"Thanks to the both of you. I'm really glad we found each other," Brie said.

Suddenly, my dad entered through the front door. Brie was nervous, and I was excited. Bellduh was a little nervous. My dad looked surprised and had a tremendous smile on his face.

"Dad, this is Brie, and the one and only Bellduh."

My dad came closer to Brie and Bellduh to greet them. He shook their hands. Brie smiled and seemed at home. Bellduh also smiled and was not as nervous anymore.

"Brie, it's a pleasure to meet you. Hello, Bellduh. Don't mind me, I just came back from a long day at work. It's a little nippy outside. Brie, you must like eating cheese. We have plenty of that around here."

Brie seemed to enjoy my dad's presence. My dad could be entertaining. Brie seemed a little too comfortable around my dad.

"Will you girls be staying for dinner? We never have enough company around here, so I think this would be the perfect opportunity."

"Yes, they will be staying for dinner. It's been kind of silent around here. Good thinking, Dad. You girls are always welcome here. We don't usually have guests over for dinner, or any guests at all. My dad will fix us a hot meal. It will be ready soon enough."

"If it's alright, Brie and Bellduh will be staying the night. It will be like a little slumber party."

My dad looked at me and smiled at the girls.

"Well, you are more than welcome to sleep over, girls. Make yourself at home, both you girls are part of the family now."

My dad was very generous and very open. He just loved guests. He was happy that I had made some friends. Brie was thankful and was very happy. She probably hadn't had this much hospitality since her last slice of cheese. I showed Brie and Bellduh around the house.

Brie seemed to really love my place. It must have been a little paradise for Brie since she probably never had this much peace in her life. I found it interesting to see how she valued our time together.

There was something kind and gentle about Brie. She loved cheese so much. You would never have guessed that she was the victim of such physical and mental abuse.

Brie should have appreciated the moment. She would have never known what would have happened in the next chapter of her life.

Bellduh and I had gotten to know Brie a little more as we waited for my dad to prepare dinner. There was a lot more to Brie that anyone would have ever known. She seemed to be a little bit mysterious.

We made our way to the dinner table. Candle lit and a cooked, hardy meal on the table and a lot of cheese.

My dad filled Brie's plate up with meat and sliced cheese. It was a lot more than she could possibly eat, but he wanted to make sure she was satisfied, since he loved to be hospitable. Bellduh didn't eat much. She seemed to be playing with her food.

It was very quiet at the table. My dad said grace. Brie was occupied with her meal. My dad and I played with our food since we only wanted blood. Brie and Bellduh do not notice.

My dad was a very unique junkie, just like me. We handed each other notes under the table so that we could talk about the situation.

"Brie and Bellduh are both sweet smelling, Edworth. I could smell their sweet blood from outside the front door. I wonder, are they really friends? Be honest with me about Bellduh," dad said.

I sipped my glass that was filled with blood. The girls thought it was red wine. Brie was taking her time eating her meal, occasionally making eye contact with my dad and I.

"I found Brie in the forest while I was with Bellduh. Truth is, I wanted to finish them both tonight after their last supper, but were not like that, but if you want to we could. Brie's life is sad and pointless, dad, no one will miss her, or even notice her gone. She is useless. I like Bellduh, but I am so tempted that I want to just taste her tonight. I'm confused and keep changing my mind about Bellduh. Everything is last minute."

"Edworth, as much as you want to drink them, you will not taste them. You need friends, and one of them loves cheese. That says a lot you know. This is not who we are anymore. You will turn them into one of us tonight. You will teach them everything, or you shall let them go, set them free, and let them on her way."

I had to make a decision. What was I going to do? Did I really want them as junkie companions? I wouldn't be lonely anymore. I wanted Bellduh to be my companion, but I wasn't sure about Brie. She loved cheese too much. It was kind of weird. I couldn't have two companions; that was just weird.

Bellduh and I could have feasted together. It would have been much easier to lure people home and feed on their blood. It could have been the beginning of a beautiful relationship.

Maybe my dad had a point. I couldn't help but think about Brie's sweet smell.

I wanted to just let Brie go, and take my chances. I didn't think that Brie would have told anyone about my place. I thought about giving her a lot of cheese to take with her.

Brie and Bellduh were done with their meals, and we had a little conversation, mostly small talk. My dad spoke of his hunting escapades, which interested Brie.

The night was long, and I had finally escorted Brie and Bellduh to their beds. We stayed up for about a couple of hours.

Bellduh and I gathered in Brie's room and told each other stories of our lives, and entertained each other with them. What Brie and Bellduh didn't know was the truth. I continued to make stories up, to keep them entertained.

What I didn't tell them was the truth about my dad and I. I would have loved to tell them about what my dad and I have done in the past.

My family and I have gone from place to place and took out whole towns together. We have had the bloodiest feasts. It didn't matter who we had feasted on. We feasted on the blood of men and women. We even fed on the blood of boys and girls, and children as well. We were very bad. We were nothing but junkies.

We did not discriminate. Any person of any race would do. They could be black, pink, white, brown, yellow, or blue. We have even feasted on dog and cats. We loved virgin blood mixed with extra virgin olive oil. We loved to feed on the rich, rather than the poor. The rich seemed to have better-tasting blood. We eventually moved on to other cities, and other towns, before people would get a chance to become suspicious of us.

We also indulged on the old and the near death. We didn't hesitate on tasting the near death. It was all the same to us. My family and I were just happy to be alive and were thankful to have blood to feed on.

We once had a small party of students at my home. My dad and I had blood that lasted a week! It was a great party. We didn't want the party to ever end. We had too much fun at our parties. We managed to get the party goers so wasted that they didn't know what happened. Tasting blood was an art, and it was life.

It was what we were. We sucked the blood out of anything and anyone. We had no shame. That was the life of us junkies. We did what was necessary to stay alive. We once finished up a family of eight together. Feeding on triplets was a beautiful experience. It was that easy. Become a junkie one day, and you will understand…

The young ones had very sweet blood. They weren't enough to satisfy our hunger though. We needed to feed on adults mostly.

We were out of control. We feasted every night of the year. It was a madhouse of blood.

As the years passed by us, we eventually took control. We slowly, but surely tasted less and less people.

We eventually lived off the blood of animals, mostly rats, and rabbits. That is just the way it was, and we are a lot more civil these days.

Brie would probably never understand. She is very lucky to have met my dad and I. Her timing was more than perfect. If Brie met us years before, she might have joined us back then.

Morning had finally arrived, and I was off to school and Brie thanked me for taking her in. She hoped that we would see each other again. I told her that we would someday.

I decide to let her go and hoped that she chose a better path. I was going to improve my life as well.

I continued to wonder about Brie. I wondered if she should be given the luxury of being a junkie. I wondered if it would be worth it.

She must have had some qualities. She would have also made a nice companion and a decent addition to my family. She still needed to explore her current life and see what life would bring her, perhaps more cheese.

If life were good to her, she would live a long life and grow old with her husband and family. Life could have also continued to be cruel to her and bring her nothing but misery.

For now, Brie needed to find more cheese for herself and to get out there and live her life the way it was meant to be lived. There was something about her, which was bizarre.

She was always welcome to my home. She could have had as much cheese as she wanted.

Act 12

I had made my way to music class. I walked into the classroom and found that blood aroma that made me very thirsty. I really, really, truly longed for Bellduh. She must have been wondering about the other night, and what a nice night it was. She turned to look at me. She looked into my eyes.

"What happened to you yesterday, Edworth? You were really into that Brie girl, and hardly into me," Bellduh asked.

"I got held up in the moment. The new girl needed my attention. I still want this to work. Let's spend more time together."

"You want to spend more time together, and that sounds good to me, Edworth."

Students took turns to get in front of the class and play their instrument's to demonstrate their own talent. I saw that Bellduh was watching the students do their thing.

I was anxious to see Bellduh play her flute.

Her lips were plump and ready to be kissed. I wondered if Bellduh would let me taste her blood anytime soon.

I wondered how things would turn out between us, and what she wanted from me. Maybe she just wanted to make out with me. I had things that I wanted to tell Bellduh. I was truly excited. We had many things to talk about. I was sure she had a lot of questions for me. I was ready to answer all of her questions.

I wished that she could have read my mind so that she knew that I love her so much, but I mostly loved her blood. I wanted to invite her over to my place again so that I could have a taste of her blood. Maybe we could have made cupcakes together. I wanted to turn Bellduh so that she could be she could be my love forever.

I could have come clean and told her how I felt. It's not like she would have hated me. If she had come to my place, we could have really gotten to know each other better, and maybe I would have been tempted to suck her blood out and hurt her. On second thought, I didn't really want to hurt Bellduh. I loved her too much. I didn't think I would have had the balls to hurt her, no matter how beautiful her blood was. I longed to have her blood in my mouth.

I wondered if just a taste of her blood was enough, or if I needed all of it. I didn't want Bellduh to be gone for good.

I wanted to turn her into a junkie like me. There was so much drama. I didn't know why I did that to myself. Girls could be nothing but trouble sometimes. Bellduh was nothing but a witch, yet I loved her deeply, though it was mostly her blood I desired.

I was very in love with Bellduh's blood, and there was nothing I would not have done for her. I was so attracted and connected to Bellduh that I would have done anything for her. I hoped that she had felt the same way. I would have walked naked in school for Bellduh. I would have licked every part of her body clean. I would have hurt every single person on earth for Bellduh until we were the only ones left in the world.

For Bellduh's bloody love, I would have hurt every junkie in the world, and I would have even hurt my family for Bellduh's blood. I would have even licked every part of Jacub Blacky's dirty body. The stench of Jacub was unbelievably unthinkable, and I would have put myself in a steam room and inhaled his deadly foul stench to prove my love for Bellduh's blood.

I would have even made a deal with the devil for Bellduh's blood. Yes, I think it was pretty much obvious how badly I wanted Bellduh's blood.

During class, the teacher had surprised us by setting the class up into teams. Suddenly, I learned that Bellduh and I were set up together. We were supposed to improvise and play our musical instruments together. I had no idea what I was going to do.

It was already our turn to play our flutes. We got ready to play. Bellduh said nothing to me.

She smiled, and I smiled back. She began to play, and I tried to follow along. It was truly so embarrassing.

I was playing my usual romantic tune, and there Bellduh was ruining everything. As I looked at the class, they were looking at Bellduh and trying not to laugh at her. Her tune was really off that day.

As I attempted to play my tune, they looked at Bellduh with dirty looks knowing that she had been ruining my lovely tune. Even the teacher knew that she had been screwing everything up. It was actually a travesty. I didn't want to listen to Bellduh's sour tune.

After another couple of minutes later, the nightmare was over. That really might have ruined my chances with Bellduh. I was a little turned off by her tune.

We had finally finished with our musical flute duo. The class was silent, and they started to slowly applaud. It's because of me that Bellduh didn't get hounded by her bad tune. Bellduh didn't even look at me as we sat back down. The next couple had stood up to play their flute. Bellduh looked at me and smiled.

"What the heck was that you were playing? It sounded like you were killing a cat," I said.

Bellduh must have thought that I was joking and just smiled as I admired Bellduh. It was finally lunch time, and I noticed Jacub was not at school that day. He was probably embarrassed about all the humiliation he had suffered. I didn't blame the guy. If I were him, I would have taken some time off school to relax.

The sun was not shining, so I decided to go outside and enjoy the outdoors as much as I could. I sat alone in the shade. Kermit saw me sitting alone and decided to join me.

"Hey Edworth, may I join you?"

I looked up and smiled while he looked down at me.

"Shouldn't you be with Roosilly today?"

"Yes Edworth, but she's out shopping right now."

Bellduh saw us and joined us as we had a conversation.

Kermit decided to indulge in his personal life. He seemed as if he had been smoking up. He seemed to have some sort of connection with Bellduh. Maybe it was my imagination. He had a very unique voice, and I think Bellduh adored him.

"So, like... you and Casper used to date right?" Bellduh asked.

"Oh Bellduh, my dear Bellduh... if you only knew," Kermit said.

Kermit decided to reminisce about his days while he dated Casper. They both had their own sides of their stories, and I never knew the real truth.

Bellduh gazed into his eyes as he spoke. She must have been imagining every romantic moment as he spoke. Kermit mentioned that it was a sunny day; the sky was blue, and the air was fresh. Casper and Kermit were having a picnic. They let out little giggles at one another. They were very much in love.

Casper and his love Kermit were the talk of the town. Anything that happened would spread like wildfire. They were local celebrities. They had the usual romantic cheese, grapes, and even red wine that created the most romantic date, yet it was all for show since they were junkies.

They used to have so much fun together. I guessed that they wanted to seem normal as much as possible. They were sitting next to each other and whispering into each other's ears as they smiled and giggled. They took turns touching each other slowly. They were like two boys in a dream, and it seemed like it was just a matter of time before they woke up.

Casper closed his eyes while Kermit touched him gently. Casper would slowly tease Kermit by touching him back and tickling him.

Kermit would love to watch Casper's lips move the way they did. As Casper stood still, Kermit would kiss Casper on the lips.

Casper would then take his fingers and put them into Kermit's mouth. It would get very intense. They were boys in love.

It was definitely a really weird relationship. Casper would be on his back while Kermit would lean over him, and they would share a passionate kiss. They would tell each other jokes and giggle. I guessed that it was romantic to them.

They would be next to each other and stare at the cloudy sky while holding hands. They would share each other's deepest secrets. They would massage each other with all kinds of scented oils, and it was very erotic. They even did odd things while oiled up.

They were full of smiles, and they were very much in love. Nothing in the world was going to stop them from loving each other. Casper seemed to be more passionate than Kermit.

Casper knew Kermit was the dominate one, and that's what he wanted. Casper was not the one to lead and take control. He expected it to come from Kermit, and it came naturally.

Together they were a team, a superpower, and a stronghold. They were one. Where one would go, the other would follow. They would sit next to each other during classes, and they would hand each other love letters and poems.

Kermit would shed tears at the love poems that Casper would write to him. Kermit was a real manly man, but very emotional when it came to Casper's love. Casper was a true poet. There was nothing in the world that could take their love away from them since it was too powerful.

Kermit was never good at writing love poems; they made Casper giggle and laugh. Casper still loved everything Kermit did for him. They bent over backwards for each other.

They would go to the movies together and make out viciously, even while people watched, cheered them on and applauded.

People would even record them with their phones while they made out, and post them online. They would run naked together in the fields while the moon was full, and the night was young. The beautiful mist would make the night much more romantic.

They would take long swims in the lake nearby. Casper and Kermit would kiss deeply while in the water.

They loved to go deep into the lake and explore. They loved to experiment. They made out underwater, and Casper wished they could have stayed underwater forever since it was away from the troubles of the real world.

They would stay out until the sun came out, and would love to watch the moon. They would take turns massaging each other. They would do pretty much anything together, including hunting for blood. They would sing to each other and make love. A romantic time at the lake would follow. They would spend a lot of time outdoors as they made love everywhere that they could. It was a very emotional time for them. They both had their deep and dirty desires.

Casper would bend over on the bedspread while Kermit would do what he did best to Casper from behind. Casper admitted that he loved every second of it.

They would take turns pleasing each other in naughty ways. They both had very different fetishes. Casper would want blood all over his body and would make Kermit lick it up. Kermit preferred Casper to dress up in a miniskirt and stilettos while acting like a hooker.

Casper wanted Kermit to tie him up, whip his butt with a belt, and then go down on him. It was very erotic. Kermit loved it when Casper would pour hot candle on his body, and then they would put blood on each other and do the unspeakable together while sucking and licking all the blood.

There was no limit to the amount of fun they had. They did many unthinkable acts together. Casper loved to do weird things with Kermit. There were many hectic nights.

There were things that Casper didn't know about Kermit. He would slowly learn the deep desires that Kermit longed for. Kermit had a fetish of having a threesome with Casper.

At first, Casper refused as he would not share Kermit with anyone in the world. Casper was offended and felt disrespected by the idea. They would argue for days about the idea.

Eventually, destiny would run its course, and Casper would give in to the unthinkable desires of Kermit. Even though they argued, Casper was in love and just could not say no, or stay upset with Kermit. Casper was first introduced to the other male who renamed nameless to Casper.

He was just another guy trying to earn an extra buck. That mysterious guy offered himself all over the town of Eclipse. Kermit had found him in an alley where Kermit would go to cheat on Casper.

Casper was nervous at first, but for Kermit's love, he opened up to have a threesome and made Kermit very happy.

The threesome went on as Kermit had his way with another guy and Casper joined in. Casper wanted to drink the guy's blood. Kermit was repulsed by the idea, and Casper just carried on.

Kermit became demanding and wanted more, and more.

Again, Casper did not have the heart to say no.

Kermit suddenly became very dominant in the relationship.

He began abusing Casper while having pleasure. Kermit decided that he wanted to make money off this insane sick idea that he revealed to Casper. He wanted Casper to offer himself out for money. Casper was furious!

Casper suffered a lot of mental abuse.

The people at Eclipse High knew things were not going well. There was no way that they would ever believe that Casper was involved in an abusive relationship with Kermit.

Kermit would doll Casper up for his nights out and offered Casper's body to other men of Eclipse.

Casper would wear makeup, a skirt, and glass stilettos. He was the perfect streetwalker. The men of Eclipse paid top dollar to have their way with Casper. Casper wanted to drink their blood, but did not.

Word got out on the streets that Casper was the best. Night after night, Casper would get used by paying men. He was very popular. Casper would show up to an all-male bar, and he would be seen as a celebrity.

He got so popular that the price of buying time with Casper went up like the price of gas. He was in demand. Only the highest bidders got the pleasure of Casper. Casper was a business that was only for a limited time only.

Casper admitted that he was thinking of hurting himself, but he couldn't stand the thought of being without Kermit. He wanted to just roast in the hot sun.

After all the mental abuse, Casper was still madly in love with Kermit.

Kermit's fetish of abusing Casper while having pleasure eventually became too much for Casper to handle. Casper was mentally unstable every night.

One night, Casper had gotten so upset, he went out and hurt a bunch of people. That was what helped him calm down. Kermit was no longer making love to Casper.

Casper felt like he was being taken for granted. He absolutely could not stand it. Casper would not give up on Kermit since he was so in love with him.

He tried to get Kermit to be the way he was, but it did not happen. Things between Casper and Kermit were way beyond redemption. Things were different, and they were too deep to reach shallow waters.

Kermit began going off on his own and continued to have pleasure with other guys. He was also tasting a lot of people.

Casper knew he was being cheated on, and again he would wait for Kermit to return to him. Somewhere deep down in Casper's soul, he suspected that it was not going to be a happy ending.

Casper had wished that Kermit would change. Casper once considered proposing to Kermit. He wondered if Kermit would have him, forever. He decided not to propose since he could not take the rejection from Kermit.

He had dreams of Kermit being the way he used to be. Kermit was at the point of no return, and Casper knew it to be true. There was nothing Casper could do to change Kermit.

Everything they had was gone. Casper still loved Kermit, but he did not love what Kermit had become.

One day, the time had come for Casper to talk to Kermit. They were broken up just like that. Casper could not take it anymore. His life was better off without the abuse that Kermit was giving him.

Everyone at Eclipse High would stare at Casper and Kermit. Rumors would haunt them for months.

Casper went into a deep depression. He was drinking a lot of rat blood. He sold his body on and off for more money, not that he really needed any money. He was in a very dark place at that point in his life. Eventually, Casper went to a very deep depression. Nothing helped much at first. Time had gone by, and Casper slowly gained his life back. It was no easy journey. Casper went through a lot of agony. He started to improve, and people noticed.

Eventually, things died down, and Casper and Kermit moved on. In the end, Casper learned a great life lesson. Nothing in the beautiful world lasted forever, especially in the town of Eclipse.

Casper would never trust another guy ever again. It was awkward since we all lived close together. Casper enjoyed the single life for a while. Being alone was one of the things that really helped him gain his dignity back. There were many things that Casper had done to gain his life back again.

He would go on long walks and took up reading. He had even taken up yoga classes. He would go to the place where he and Kermit would swim.

Casper didn't care that the lake reminded him of Kermit. He enjoyed the peaceful waters. He actually recovered mentally in the waters. It soothed his soul and relaxed his mind.

Kermit wasn't as bothered by the ordeal as Casper was. He took it like a man and just didn't care. Casper was the very emotional one that had a heart and soul.

Casper eventually moved on. He and Alicia had developed a relationship while they were in the freak show together back in the old days. He continued to date Alicia, and things were beautiful with them. Casper will never be as happy as he was when he was with Kermit.

"That's very sad to hear Kermit, but I'm happy for you now. You found someone better for you," Bellduh said.

"Thank you, Bellduh. I am very happy with Roosilly. She has a lot of respect for me. No abuse, no crazy drama, just peace and love."

Kermit, Bellduh and I, just sat in the shade and enjoyed the rest of our lunch break. The day went on, and I couldn't wait to get home. Bellduh and I needed to talk. I was very determined. We really needed to talk about how things were developing and express our feelings.

Act 13

I had made my way to school, and everyone was hanging out outside and I saw that Bellduh was with her friends. They looked like they were up to no good. I was not in the mood for anyone that day. I just wanted to get that day over with. I wondered what could possibly go wrong.

I took my time walking towards the school. I felt like everyone outside was watching me, but they really weren't. I had no idea who I wanted to talk to. I just minded my own business, then and continued on my way. I took out my books and made it like I was trying to study. Figured that I could avoid everyone and not draw much attention. Bellduh just needed a little time before we spoke again since she seemed distant.

I saw Jacub walking in the parking lot. He looked like he was checking out cars. He looked like he wanted to vandalize everyone's car. Kermit was racing his way into the parking lot. Wow, he was driving way out of control. I wondered if he planned on slowing down. Kermit was driving pretty fast. It looked like he was losing control of his vehicle. Jacub was in his raging path. It was an accident waiting to happen. I needed to do something fast.

Suddenly, Kermit started to lose control of his car. I saw that Jacub was in his path.

"Jacub! Watch out! Get out of the way!" I shouted.

Instead of getting out of the way, Jacub looked at me and smiled. What a dork. He was so dumb, and I distracted him from the car that was aiming right for him. Jacub turned at the last second to see Kermit's car rushing towards him.

I used my junkie speed to jump in front of Jacub. I pushed Jacub to the ground, and Kermit's car ended up stopping and just missed the two of us. I wondered if Kermit was going to lose his driver's license. He did not deserve to be driving.

Everyone rushed to the scene. A lot of students were taking pictures with their phones. I wondered if anyone really cared about our safety. They seemed more concerned about taking pictures and posting them online. They were all just a bunch of animals. It was like a zoo. I didn't see students surrounding us. I saw sheep, monkeys, apes, dogs, cats, bears, and rats. What a jungle Eclipse High was. I didn't think that anyone had any respect for anyone around here.

For some reason, not one person even saw me rush to Jacub, except for him.

People were asking Jacub if he was ok, and not one person even noticed me. This was just not my day at all. I guessed that Jacub would have all the attention. I don't know what it was about the school parking lot that was always so dangerous. People were just so careless and didn't know how to drive.

Jacub was on the ground. He looked like he was using that opportunity to get everyone's attention. Someone like Jacub loved that kind of special attention. He looked like he was still stunned at what happened. I wondered if anyone saw me save Jacub's worthless life. I was sure that several people saw me. However, I wasn't sure if they saw me save Jacub. I would have liked some attention for being a hero.

Jacub looked at me like he had seen a ghost. There was no doubt that he suspected I did something to save his life. I didn't think that he knew for sure. Jacub was a mystery most of the time.

"Come on, get up! Be a man, Jacub!" I said.

Jacub smiled.

Kermit rushed to the scene. He pretended to care. I knew that he was a total fake.

"Jacub! You ok?" I'm so sorry! God, please don't scare me like that man!" Kermit said.

Jacub smiled as practically everyone in the school looked on.

"Ya... I'm fine now. Thanks for asking," Jacub said.

"See, he's fine. Nothing to see here," I said.

People started to disperse and started laughing. I smiled and looked around. As I looked around, I saw Bellduh staring at me from across the crowd. I gave her a half smile and nodded as if to say hello.

She looked at me and did the same. She turned away slowly and walked away into the school. The rest of the day was weird. I had spent the school day watching Bellduh. I wondered if she had witnessed my odd talent. She might have thought that I was showing off.

Bellduh didn't say much in class. It was more like she looked at me funny and some small talk. I was trying to figure out Bellduh's mysterious ways.

I still wondered if Jacub noticed my strange speed. There was no way anyone in the world could have gotten to him that fast. He was still in shock, and the time was eventually going to come when he would have made sense of it all.

School was finally out for the day. It was such a long day. I had started to make my way home. As I got to the field that I walked through every day, a strong stench was approaching. It was Jacub, of course.

"Edworth! Wait up!" he shouted.

I'm not sure what was on his mind, since I couldn't seem to read everyone's thoughts for some odd reason, but I tried. I slowed down for Jacub. I took a deep breath and got ready for some stinky feet, or maybe this time it was going to be a smelly butt after taking a dump and not wiping his butt.

"Jacub, how are you feeling?"

Jacub smiled and then giggled like a girl.

"That was like, so intense. My heart practically flew out of my body," he said.

"You looked like you were checking out the cars in the parking lot. Did you see anything interesting?"

"How nice of you to notice, Edworth. I saw a few interesting rides. I was thinking of buying a car. I just wanted to see what the cool people were driving."

"Yes, it was like so close to death for you. I guess Kermit should like, learn how to drive."

"He is so clumsy. Someone should take away his license and give him a bike to ride."

We continued to walk slowly together and talk. We approached the dark forest. Jacub really stunk, but I decided to be polite.

"Are you coming with me, Jacub?"

"Sure, why not? I like the dark forest, don't you, Edworth? It kind of comes naturally to me."

88

"It's a nice forest. It's peaceful. Why does it come naturally to you, Jacub?"

"Well, it's where my family was raised. They were pretty much raised in the wild, in forests, you know, the wilderness."

"Well, this is my stop, Jacub. Home sweet home."

"Edworth, I just wanted to ask you something. How did you get to me so fast today? I don't remember you being close enough too…

Suddenly, my dad opened the front door.

"Hey kids! Who is this guy, Edworth? New friend, maybe?" he giggled.

"You must be Mr. Cuddles. I'm Jacub Blacky, Edworth's school friend. He, uh… practically saved my life today."

"You are truly lucky that Edworth was there, Jacub."

That moment was so cheesy. I wished that it had ended really fast since I hated awkwardness. Everyone seemed so normal, except for me. I hated the awkward silence because it just killed me, even if it was only for a couple of seconds. Jacub's stench was really getting to me. I wished that my dad took a hint and got Jacub to leave. I couldn't take it anymore; I tried to move my lips and hoped that my dad could read my words.

"Please dad, make him go away, far away from here, like right now. He stinks."

My dad read my lips, but didn't respond, and decided to tease me.

"Are you coming inside, Jacub?"

Oh no, he had just invited Jacub inside! He was obviously playing with my emotions.

"Oh no, no. Thank you, Mr. Cuddles. That's very thoughtful of you. However, I should get going. It was very nice to meet you, Sir."

"The pleasure is always mine, Jacub. I hope to see you again sometime."

"Edworth, I will see you at school. Well, talk soon," Jacub said.

"See you soon, Jacub. Have a good night," I said.

Jacub made his way back home. I entered my home, and my dad, and I sat in front of the fireplace. I give my dad the evil eye, then a smile.

"Wow, what in the heck was that stink, Edworth?"

"That would be Jacub, of course. Isn't he such a repellant?"

My dad continued to tell me how bad the smell was. He couldn't stop giggling at how bad the smell was.

In fact, my dad told me that he would have invited Jacub over for dinner just to make me suffer, so he could have a good laugh about it after.

My dad started to make jokes about the whole thing. He told me cheesy knock-knock jokes about Jacub, and about how much he stunk.

I have to admit that the jokes were pretty funny.

There was a lot of cheesiness that night at Jacub's expense. Even at dinner, my dad just did not let the jokes go. I loved spending those times with my dad. The moments were priceless.

My dad had the best sense of humor in the world. I wished everyone was as happy as he was. No one could have replaced my dad.

It was probably going to be a traditional thing since my dad had met Jacub. He was never going to let the jokes go. There was nothing I could do about it. I just had to laugh with my dad as he continued with the jokes.

The weekend had finally arrived, and I had nothing to do, but hunt for blood. My dad was with me since he had never had anything better to do with himself. He always told me to make friends, and I always told him that I was working on it.

I really didn't want to hang out with anyone that weekend, and Bellduh was having her mood swings.

My dad was the one that found another junkie to turn me when I was thirsty. He wouldn't do it himself since he was afraid to catch a disease. He just happened to save me on time. I was forever thankful. My dad was turned way before me.

He was part of this Voltweety circus act that he ran away from and had claimed that he was hunted by them ever since he had decided to get away from them. They were more amazing than he was.

He never really got into the story with me, but I knew he was part of it, and he didn't like to talk about it. We could smell that there was something smelly approaching us as we wandered deep into the dark forest. We had suddenly come upon a smelly old man. He was tall and kind of looked like Jacub. They must have been related. The nasty stench gave it all away.

"You're a long way from home, my friends," the old man said.

"Hello, Sir. My son and I live just minutes away from here."

"I'm Silly Blacky. This is my territory that you walk on."

"You must be related to Jacub Blacky? He is a friend of mine from school," I said.

"Well, well, so you know Jacub. Any friend of Jacub is a friend of mine. You're welcome here, my friends. Just make sure to not harm any wildlife. They are like family to me and my family."

My dad let out a smile.

"Oh well, we wouldn't dare. We were just out getting some air. I don't spend enough time with my son, Edworth. It's a beautiful day in the neighborhood, don't you think?"

Silly Blacky looked at my dad suspiciously.

"Yes, it is a beautiful day. Well, you take care now. Maybe I will see you again sometime," Silly Blacky said.

"Nice to meet you, Sir," I said.

Silly Blacky walked away whistling a tune and wandered off.

My dad and I started to walk back, and we did not say much to each other. I guessed that my dad wanted to break the silence since he continued with the stinky jokes.

"Wow, did he ever stink," he said.

We laughed, and my dad kept up the stinky jokes all the way home.

The next day, I had decided to go into town. I wanted to just get out. Nothing much was happening in town.

Suddenly, there were a few drunken guys ahead of me.

I could smell them. They smelled like bad cheese. I had crossed the street to avoid any kind of trouble. It was too late since they had seen me crossing, and they followed me. They demanded to know what I was up to and where I was going. There were about a dozen of them.

They must have been part of the football team or something. Most of them seemed athletic and were obviously looking for a fight. If they had only known who I was. They saw me as their next victim of mental abuse, but that was not going to happen.

I could have easily run from them, but I was sick of being different. I didn't do anything different from normal people. I did exactly what the next person would have done, which was to just walk faster.

They finally decided to run, and they surrounded me. It was like a bunch of dogs were ready for their midnight snack or something.

"Where are you off to? Got any money?" the drunk guy murmured.

"Look guys, I just want to go home."

"Well, give us all your money and we will let you go? We just want money."

They all continued to drink and blab on as if I cared what they had to say. Honestly, I could have tasted all of them in just a few seconds if I wanted to. I could have tasted them in a heartbeat. It had come close to that.

Unless I had seriously needed to hurt them, I was not going to. I wanted to just play it out and toy with them. The smell of the blood on some of them was tempting me to taste them right away. I was just trying to be like everyone else, so I decided to stick with the plan.

"Look guys, I really don't want to hurt any of you, tonight. Therefore, why don't you all just go away. Just go home and play with yourselves," I said.

They all had a good laugh. Some of them were on the ground, and too drunk to get back up.

"HEY! GET AWAY FROM HIM!" Jacub yelled.

The drunken guys took off, and I was saved. Jacub was with his gang of smelly friends. What a coincidence that was. I wanted to avoid him, but he saw me. Jacub must have been wondering what I was doing there all alone. I had to face the music.

"Edworth! Where are you going? What were you doing with those losers?" Jacub asked.

I turned around and smiled.

"Jacub, I was just taking a walk."

Jacub approached me, leaving his buddies behind him. We continued to walk together. Obviously, his stench made those guys run away in terror. He talked about how drunk he had gotten the night before. He just loved to brag. We found a nice place to sit down in the park. There was no one around. It was not exactly how I planned the night. I just had to deal with it.

"Looks like you owe me one, Edworth. I have been doing a lot of thinking, and I have decided that I'm in love with Bellduh," Jacub said.

I giggled like a girl at Jacub.

"I want you to get to know Bellduh better. It's really her decision on who she wants to be with," I said.

"Edworth, I just want you to know that I saw everything."

"What did you see?"

"It may not have looked like I was watching you outside, but I had my eye on you. I was watching you from the moment you arrived, and I saw what you did."

My mouth dropped as Jacub claimed to have seen me make the move to save him from being smashed to death.

"I don't know what you saw, but whatever you say, Jacub."

"What are you, Edworth? You seem different."

"I can tell you what you saw was me running like the wind to get to you, Jacub. That's really all it was."

I was not ready to tell Jacub, the truth about myself. The timing wasn't right. I had waited to see what would happen. I knew it was killing him inside. He demanded to know what it was about me that was special, but that night was not the right time.

"I know what I saw, Edworth."

"I don't know what you saw, Jacub. It must have been your imagination."

"It must have been. Well, there was a moment where I couldn't see you, when the car was blocking my view. I guess it was your lucky day, and I must have been seeing things. You know, Edworth, the eyes can play tricks on you sometimes," Jacub said.

"Yes the eyes can play very bad tricks on you if you let them. I should get going now. I wouldn't want my dad to worry since I'm a very delicate young lad."

"Ok, Edworth. Be more careful where you walk next time."

I made my way out of the park and was on my way home.

The night had soon turned to daylight, and it was another day at school. I made my way to the outside of the school, and it was another odd day. The same faces greeted me as I made my way closer to the school.

Bellduh was with her weird friends, and saw me with a smile, and Jacub was admiring her from afar.

Every single day was a tale to be told. Derek Yucky, who was the only Asian kid at school, approached Bellduh. He was in our music class. That day, his hair was pure white with green stripes, and it was odd looking. I disliked his piercings. He had started to hang out with Michael Angelo Shakespeare Knewton for some strange reason. Derek Yucky started to talk to Bellduh. I tried to read Bellduh's lips to figure out the conversation. I was impressed with how good I was at reading lips.

"Bellduh Swansinner, how are you? I'm Derek, Derek Yucky. I haven't had the pleasure of meeting you. We are in the same music class together."

"Yes, Derek. I have seen you around. You hang out with Michael Angelo Shakespeare Knewton," Bellduh said.

"Yes, that's right. He is such a poet. I am very fond of him."

Derek was also part of the drama club. Him and his other unusual friends went around taking all kinds of pictures. They loved to spread rumors.

They were like the paparazzi of the school. He could have taken a picture of you, and you wouldn't have known.

"Well, it's very nice to meet you, Derek. I'm just going to head off to class now," Bellduh said.

Derek grabbed her arm to get my attention, I bet.

"Before you go, Bellduh, I just want to give you this package with photos. Have a look at them on your spare time, and let me know what you think. My number is in this envelope. You don't have to open it now, just take your time, and when you're on break have a look. Let me know your opinion. Thanks, Bellduh," Derek said.

Bellduh accepted the package and waited to open it. Derek walked away, and I made my way to my class.

The day was long, and all I thought about all day was Bellduh.

I walked into Biology class. Bellduh sat beside me. Obviously, she missed me. I smiled at Bellduh as Casper watched us.

"Bellduh, I hope today is satisfying for you," Casper said.

"Thanks, I guess."

"Bellduh, how's it going today? You look really nice, I mean like... you look the same, well you know," I said.

This was like totally awkward. That was so not cool of me. I was such a dork for saying that. I was supposed to be cool. Bellduh was watching me like a hawk. She made things feel awkward. It had been an intense class. Every time I saw Bellduh, it felt like we had just met.

"Thanks. You look great today, Edworth," Bellduh said.

Bellduh just stared at me. I just minded my own business for a couple of moments, and I noticed her still staring at me. The moment was so odd.

"So... I saw you talking with Jacub Blacky. He must have the biggest crush on you, Edworth," Bellduh joked.

"That kid is a joke; he's like the town fool and is like obsessed with me or something. He's also buddies with the Dirtywaters, who are just as stinky as Jacub," I said.

"Well, that's very true. They really stink a lot. You don't have to tell me that. Being a stinky person doesn't make you a bad person. It's just going to make your life miserable in the long run."

"Come on, Bellduh, we've smelled Jacub. Jacub stinks like armpits and gravy with rotten eggs. He's like a total wreck. I tell you what Bellduh, come with me, and we can give Jacub a bath."

"Edworth, that is like so thoughtful of you. Jacub could use a good bath. He needs to get the best soaps that money can buy. We should do it, and I'm sure he will love it."

Bellduh smiled, and I giggled at the idea.

"Bellduh, that sounds like a plan. Jacub and I are somewhat buddies. He really does need a cleaning. He might just get more popular around school if he cleans himself up. I'm sure his friends could use a good cleaning as well."

"That sounds great, Edworth. I know he will change his ways and clean his act up. I'm sure he will let us. I have just the thing that will help Jacub get all cleaned up. I'm sure I will be doing him a favor, but I won't let you know just yet what it is, Edworth."

Bellduh smiled and offered her hand. I shook her hand and smiled.

"It's a deal," I said.

I had a feeling that I had just made a deal with the devil. Little did Bellduh know, that I was suspicious of her. I was going to find out about her spells that she had used on people. Bellduh was so tempting, though it was her blood that I really wanted. She was like a forbidden fruit. She was just like a banana or mango. She was dangerous, but dangerous in a good way. I hoped that things would turn out the way that I wanted them to. I always got what I wanted, and Bellduh's blood was what I wanted badly, but I had to get passed Bellduh in order to be with the erotic scent of her blood.

The teacher had walked into the classroom, and we began class. Just for the record, I had taken Biology class hundreds of times, and I had fallen asleep every class. I really didn't know much about anything regarding Biology. That day we learned about onions, potatoes, metaphasing, protasers, phasers, or something like that, and animal phases or something. I was really lost in Biology class. I would rather have learned about blood. Now that would have been more like it. There was nothing like a bloody good lesson.

We had taken turns examining the slide of specimens through the scope.

Bellduh and I began to impress each other by pretending to know more than we did about Biology.

"You know Bellduh, I heard mouse's actually have little thingy's and mustaches. Did you know that?" I asked.

"Like, yes, I knew that for sure. Did you know that spiders have like two eyes and green feet? Bellduh asked.

I was stunned and really had no idea about spiders.

"Really? There is no way spiders have two eyes and green feet. I thought spiders had only one eye and a dozen legs. That is so weird."

Bellduh giggled.

"No, no, like they really do have two eyes and green feet. I read it in an article," Bellduh said.

I laughed. Bellduh also let out some spit as she laughed. It landed on my lips, and I licked it. It tasted like her blood, and I was excited to have a taste after waiting for so long to try.

"So… do you like bird heads?" I asked.

"Bird heads? You're asking me about bird heads? Well, I don't mind bird heads. I heard some people like to slap bird heads and even chop them up."

"Do you like to eat cat food, Bellduh?" I asked.

Bellduh smiled. The whole conversation was so random and odd. We were really getting to know each other. I wasn't sure what kind of twisted day I was having.

"Cat food is like… for losers. I would never eat that. That's like so gross, Edworth."

"What about pie, do you even like pie, like maybe blueberry pie?" I asked.

"Pie? Well, I like to eat pie when it has like apples and stuff in it. Do you even eat pie, Edworth?"

"Have you even seen my abs, Bellduh? Do I look like someone that eats pie? Wait, don't answer that," I smiled.

"You're right, Edworth. Pie can make you very fat, especially if you eat too much of it. I'm sure one piece won't hurt you, Edworth. You should try a piece of pie, like apple pie."

"I suppose I could try a small piece of pie. I think we should get together and make a pie together, Bellduh. We could make peanut butter pie if that sounds good to you."

"That sounds like a plan. I might add crushed peanuts with it. I heard dogs love peanut butter. They love to lick it up. Have you ever seen a dog's tongue up close, Edworth?"

"Are you talking about Jacub's tongue? It's probably sticky and smelly."

Bellduh smiled. I was very chatty that day. I thought that Bellduh loved that side of me. Everyone at Eclipse should have been just like me, on second thought, I don't think so. That never ever would have happened on my watch. There could only be one Edworth Cuddles.

"We should cook dinner sometime, Edworth. I know you probably don't eat much since you're so thin. Maybe you can come to my place, and I can watch you fix me up some grilled cheese sandwiches with pickles. I would love to watch you cook for me. It would be nice."

I smiled at Bellduh. I needed cooking lessons, but I was going to try.

"That really sounds like a plan, Bellduh. Ordering Chinese food would be better, even pizza, maybe."

"You just don't want to cook for me. I understand completely. It's ok; I don't like burnt food anyways, Edworth. Maybe we can go hunting. We can go to the dark forest and hurt some rabbits. Ever eat rabbit meat and drink their blood?" Bellduh asked.

My mouth dropped. I guess I was just so excited that Bellduh was on the right track. Bellduh was so awesome, and I could have done a happy dance right in front of everyone. It just felt right. Nothing has ever felt more right.

"Bellduh you're so awesome. Rabbit hunting sounds great. Drinking their blood is great. I'm down if you're down and it sounds like a plan."

Bellduh smiled. I could have pretty much said anything, and she would have been down for it. This was very exciting for me. I hoped that she was as excited as I was during that beautiful moment.

"Rabbits are so cute; I feel bad about it. However, all they ever do is linger around the dark forest. They are kind of like cats. They make great yummy meat, and I heard they would be great in a stew," Bellduh said.

"We could play checkers, chess, and you can eat gummy bears if you like that kind stuff," I said.

"Yummy. That sounds really good. Do you like hairy dwarfs? They are like so adorable." Bellduh asked.

"Dwarfs? Well, I never met one, but I guess I could try to like them. What certain things do you like and hate, Bellduh?"

"Hmm, well, I really hate stickers. They are like totally embarrassing, especially when they are on your school binders. I hate calculators, rotten potatoes, hot sauce and dirty socks. I love when guys shave their backs and crotches. I hate wasted guys. There is nothing like a great boiled egg with bacon and baked chocolate chip cookie with whipped cream."

Bellduh and I were really into our conversation. We were really getting to know each other even though we were learning such crazy things. I pretty much would have said anything for the sake of conversation. I told Bellduh what I liked and hated.

"I hate Mexican dogs, love fine wining and dining, and hate hot girls with rotten fish breath. I hate fat little pigs, and Chinese cats that don't know how to behave. I can't stand walruses, hairy fish, onion rings, sugar daddies, and sugar babies."

"Wow, that's like, so cool," Bellduh said.

"Bellduh, some of my family and I are going to La Shove Me later on today if you would like to join us. I think you were interested in it before. We're going to play some volleyball. I want you to come with me. You will love it at La Shove Me. Everyone goes there and shove each other around for fun while trying to play volleyball," I said.

"La Shove Me? That sounds like a blast. I will love to play some volleyball, Edworth. I'm really excited."

"Sounds like a plan, Bellduh. Meet me at the park around five o'clock. I will take you from there. You already know some of the members of my family, and they would love to have you there. It's going to be a blast."

"Cool, I will be there."

Class finally ended, and it was an interesting class. We learned a lot about onions, bad breath, potatoes and all kinds of crazy things. I got to know Bellduh a lot more. I hoped to get to know more about her. That was so awesome.

The lunch break approached. I looked forward to seeing everyone. Jacub was probably going to be around, stinking up the place. I could not get used to his stench.

I made my way to the cafeteria. I saw Jacub in the cafeteria. I was surprised to see him socializing with other people. This could have been the beginning of a very beautiful circle of friends. I hoped that things turned out the way that I hoped.

I made my way to Bellduh, and I sat with her when Alicia approached.

"Bellduh! I missed you!" Alicia shouted.

Alicia hugged Bellduh, and we took a walk outside the cafeteria. We went outside for some fresh air. It was nice and cloudy outside. Alicia loved gossiping. I was curious to what she had to gossip about that day.

Any rumor that went around came from Alicia most of the time. Her stories were pretty crazy, and I didn't know whether to believe them or not.

"So like, did you hear about Roosilly and Kermit?" Alicia asked.

"No... what about them?" Bellduh said.

Alicia started telling us about what happened during the weekend with Roosilly and Kermit. They were at a house party, and Michael Angelo Shakespeare Knewton was there. Everyone was there, and Kermit ended up getting it on with Michael Angelo Shakespeare Knewton since he was so wasted, and Kermit took advantage of him.

Not only did they get it on, but someone caught it on camera. Michael Angelo Shakespeare Knewton was flirting with Kermit all night long. The bad part was that Roosilly caught them messing around, but she still wanted to keep her relationship with Kermit.

It was a total mess. The weird thing was that they all went about their business as if it had never happened. I guess that's what happens when you get carried away with too much to drink.

Alicia continued to babble on about that night of craziness, and I had heard enough. However, I humored her and pretended to be interested.

The day had gone by smoothly. I was anxious to meet up with my family at La Shove Me to play a little volleyball with Bellduh. It was a great opportunity for me to get to know Bellduh better, and she could have gotten to know my family. I hoped that they liked her, and I hoped that she liked them. Bellduh and I approached La Shove Me, and I saw my family goofing around. Bellduh was happy to be there and greet my so-called family.

"Bellduh! I'm so happy you decided to come," I said.

"I wasn't going to miss it for the world," Bellduh said.

Bellduh was happy to see my so-called family together. They greeted Bellduh with smiles. Roosilly greeted Bellduh with a fake smile.

There were faces that were not familiar to Bellduh. I introduced them. They were our guests, Lowrentz, Jimmy, Zicktoria and this girl named Stephenie. There were also several others that were there to play. Bellduh recognized most of them from school.

"Everyone, I would like you to meet Bellduh Swansinner. Some of you have already met Bellduh. She is expecting a friendly game of volleyball today. Don't shove her too hard. I hope we can all get along," I smirked.

"Bellduh, it is a pleasure to meet you, I am Lowrentz. I'm from Jamaica, man. You are such a pale girl, like a ghost, man. I guess you don't get out much. Maybe you should take a trip with me to Jamaica, man," Lowrentz said.

"Please to meet you, Lowrentz. I'm very white, and you're right, I don't get out much," Bellduh said.

Lowrentz was a really nice junkie. He was really short. I practically towered over him. He must be about five feet tall. He was indeed, a really short junkie. He was very friendly. He was the most interesting junkie that I've ever met. There was just something about him that was inviting and intriguing. I heard he loved blood that had the scent of sugarcane. I bet he wouldn't have minded having a taste of Bellduh, but I knew that I wouldn't let that happen. We were much more civilized than before.

Lowrentz was topless, with shorts, and he wasn't wearing shoes. He was very athletic.

"I'm Jimmy. It's nice to meet you, Bellduh. I've heard a lot about you from Edworth. This is my twin sister, Zicktoria."

"Great to meet you guys. Looks like it might rain," Bellduh said.

Jimmy was an interesting junkie. He had tattoos all over his body. He had this look on his face like he wanted to smell you all day and all night long. He looked at Bellduh as if he wanted to smell every ounce of her. He looked just like a drug dealer high on meth. He and Zicktoria both spoke with German accents.

He still gave me the creeps though. Jimmy was very thin, white with dyed pink hair in a ponytail. He was very soft-spoken.

He was looking at me with a smile because he wanted to taste Bellduh.

Zicktoria had straight white hair with a lot of makeup on. She was in no way dressed for volleyball. It looks like she was ready to go clubbing. She was very glamorous. She was definitely ready to pose for the cover of a magazine.

"Yes, Bellduh. It really does look like the rain is coming," Zicktoria said.

Jimmy inhaled as he stood beside me. It was as if he snorted cocaine since he kept sniffing. Obviously, he loved the smell of Bellduh.

"Bellduh, you smell fine. What perfume is that? Smells very… unique," Jimmy said.

"I don't recall the name of it. It's some French name. I think it's called Aux de Ou La La," Bellduh said.

"I'm Stephenie. You look familiar Bellduh. Have we met before?"

I wondered who Stephenie was. She was kind of weird. She seemed very nice and was very young. She somehow didn't seem like she belonged here. There was something familiar about her. I couldn't seem to figure out what is was about her that interested me. She was an unusual junkie.

"There really is something familiar about you, Stephenie. I don't think I've ever seen you before. Nice to meet you," Bellduh said.

"Perhaps, we have met before. Must have been in another life," Stephenie said.

"That's another story; I guess. Your name, Stephenie, is a familiar name. I can't explain it, but it's like we've met before. That's so funny," Bellduh said.

"Life is weird. Let the games begin," Stephenie said.

Everyone started to get into positions.

"Let's get this game started!" I shouted.

The game started, and Bellduh really had no idea what she was doing. I still wanted to see if she has any skills. We were playing, and it was time to have fun. Everyone started to shove each other and faces were in the sand.

Bellduh had the pleasure of serving the ball. The rain started to pour down as we played. As I slammed the volleyball, with my fist, I slammed Zicktoria in the head, and she fell. She did not take it hard and just giggled.

Casper was swift to hit the volleyball as Bellduh served. He smashes the ball and sand exploded in everyone's face. I was happy for him. Roosilly was pretty useless. She should have stayed in a corner and admired herself in a mirror the whole game.

Roosilly was just standing around whining about everything. She couldn't even serve the volleyball. She could have at least tried to get the ball over the net. She really sucked at volleyball. She just wanted to show off her pretty nails.

Kermit and Casper seemed to be alright around each other. Lowrentz was a great server. He kept sucking on his sugarcane. He was not good at stopping the volleyball. Everyone had their own strength and weaknesses. My only weakness was the scent of Bellduh's blood.

Kermit demonstrated his power in every department. He was like a machine. Bellduh continued to serve the volleyball right. We eventually didn't care to count points any longer. We just wanted to have fun, and so we did. We loved to shove each other.

Jimmy and I crashed into each other trying to stop Casper's serve. I actually managed to land face first in the sand. Everyone was here to play, and there was a lot of competition between the guys and the girls. It was all about who was the best junkie. Everyone knew that I was the best player. I knew how to shove properly. Playing volleyball at La

Shove Me really brought out the ego in everyone.

It was really cut throat. We were all still having a great time.

"Bellduh, you're up! Serve them that volleyball nice and hard," I said.

Suddenly, out of nowhere, Jacub and his posse approached us.

The game was done. We all gathered up and stood together to see Jacub approaching. He had the volleyball that Bellduh just hit out of the boundaries. I stood close to Bellduh. Everyone was anxious to leave since the stench was so bad, but we didn't want to be rude.

"I think this volleyball belongs to someone here. It was on my property," said Jacub.

Lowrentz took the volleyball from Jacub's hand as Jacub handed it to him.

"Really, man? I had no idea that was your property, man. It will not happen again, my friend," Lowrentz said.

"So… it looks like you were having fun, playing some volleyball. Could you use some extra players?" Jacub asked.

"We all were just finishing our game. It's raining out and were all on our way home," I said.

"That's too bad. I got a sweet serve," Jacub said.

Jacub and his friends really stunk. I wished that they had left, but they didn't. We decided to leave since the stink was too much to bare. They ruined our fun. Jacub gave me a fake smile. Things had seemed a little tense. He knew exactly why we wanted to leave.

"I get it. The smell is too much for ya'll. Well, enjoy the rain and remember to keep the volleyball off my property. We will be going now. Enjoy the rain," Jacub said.

"Same to you, and come back anytime," Zicktoria said.

Jacub and his buddies walked away and went back from where they came from, as we all prepared to leave. The game of volleyball didn't last long, but we still had fun while it lasted.

Jacub's stench combined with his buddies was the most unbearable combination of stench known to mankind.

There was just no way any of us could have been able to last several minutes playing volleyball with Jacub and his smelly gang. Someone had mercy on all of us that day. Jacub was gone away, but he may have been back to play another day.

Everyone at La Shove Me was thankful to see him leave. I could tell by the desperate look in their eyes.

Act 14

One day after school was done, Bellduh met up with me. She asked if she could go over to my place and hang out. I wanted to take her to one of my cottages instead. We should have gone there and had fun.

My cottage was in another part of the dark forest. It was on the opposite side of where people lived. It was very appealing on the outside. There were a lot of windows, and it looked awesome. I looked forward to hanging out with Bellduh. We walked inside the cottage, and it looked empty.

"What do you think of my cottage, Bellduh?"

"It's very beautiful. I'm surprised at how nice it is."

We had a seat on the couch. The room was nice and romantic. We started to talk about school and about the people there. We sat for a couple of hours and had meaningful conversations.

The front door opened...

"Urethra! How are you?" I asked.

"I'm fine now that you're here," Urethra said.

"Bellduh, this is Urethra, my crazy cousin from Canada.

Bellduh greeted her with a warm smile and open arms.

"Bellduh, welcome to our cottage. I'm Urethra Cuddles. I was adopted, obviously. I haven't seen you before. I hope to see more of you. You smell good by the way. I'm a vaginal nurse up in the north by the way."

Bellduh smiled at Urethra.

"Yes, Bellduh always smells so good," I said.

Urethra continued to small talk. Bellduh must have thought that she was like so interesting. Just when I thought I was alone with Bellduh, Urethra had to interrupt.

Urethra was beautiful like me, like the female version of me. She smiled more than I did. Her personality was on the ball. She was very charming and warm. She was a catch, and she was a lesbian. If only she weren't my crazy cousin. I wanted to be alone with Bellduh, and she made things awkward. Bellduh had some sort of a girl crush on her. Urethra's eyes were friendly, sparkling red, and tempting. We were distant cousins, so I didn't mind admiring her.

Her lips were red and plump. Her face was bold, and her body was very fit. I bet that Bellduh would have loved to experience her. I wondered if Urethra noticed how perfect Bellduh's blood was.

Urethra was really someone I could trust. I knew that she was really starting to lust for Bellduh's bloody sweet blood, and I knew what she was thinking. Her eyes did not lie.

I wondered what Bellduh was thinking. I couldn't really read minds; I just got lucky all the time and pretended to be someone that I wasn't. I was trying to be the one with the cool power. I had hoped that the truth would not get out into the open. I was like the only one in my family that didn't have a special gift. I was only perfect, of course.

Urethra was truly the hottest junkie, next to me, of course. She was the hottest vaginal junkie nurse up in Canada.

Bellduh was mesmerized by her. Bellduh looked like she wanted to pay a visit to the vaginal clinic just to stare into Urethra's red eyes. That would have been a real treat for Urethra since she could have savored the scent of Bellduh's beautiful cotton candy blood.

I felt really bad by my thoughts, but they were just thoughts. I couldn't help but think the way I did. I was truly evil, at least I thought I was, but I suppose I really wasn't. I don't make any sense sometimes. It was not like I could control how I felt about blood. I am what I am, a junkie, of course.

Urethra had finally left Bellduh and I alone. I took Bellduh to my room so that I could show her around.

This should have been very interesting. We walked into my bedroom. I loved every second of it.

"Well Bellduh, how do you like my room?" I asked.

My room was very messed up. I had my socks and underwear all over the floor. My action figures were all over the place. Bellduh must have thought that I was such a slob.

Bellduh had probably never pictured my bedroom would look like a disaster. After seeing how I was at school, she probably pictured my room being perfect.

It didn't even smell like socks in my bedroom.

My bed was large and was very cozy. I had a zebra-striped blanket covering my bed. I never slept, but I still loved to get cozy on my bed. Bellduh seemed very intrigued at that point.

I showed her what I liked to do in my spare time. I was practicing for the Black Swan auditions, so I told her that did ballet dancing, and I had violin music that I was about to play for Bellduh. I pulled out my ballet shoes from underneath my bed as if they were hiding from the world. I also put on my leotards for Bellduh.

Bellduh must have been wondering who I really was. She would never have guessed.

"I used to play my drums, but I stopped playing since I got bored of it," I said.

"What are you going to play for me, Edworth?"

"Lie down on my bed and make yourself cozy, Bellduh. I'm going to surprise you with something nice."

I stood up, and Bellduh got comfortable on my bed. I got my ballerina music ready, and I was about to dance like no one was watching while I wore my tight ballet outfit.

Bellduh had a serious look on her face. She took this very seriously. All this from someone I didn't take too seriously since I just wanted her blood in my mouth.

A romantic tune played while I slowly lost myself in a dance. I closed my eyes and opened them occasionally to look deep into Bellduh's eyes.

I was very passionate as I admired her innocence. I couldn't believe that I was doing my thing in front of Bellduh.

This was very romantic and very tense. I thought that Bellduh wanted to make love. I bet she was slowly undressing me with her eyes.

As I danced as if no one was watching, I had pictured the room filled with a romantic mist to set the mood. Bellduh looked very aroused at my dance movements. It was as if I was speaking to Bellduh through my dancing.

I loved every moment of it. I was very excited to please Bellduh. I through my legs in the air and I was perfect.

She probably wished that I would have stopped dancing and just got it on with her. I wished that I could have sucked on Bellduh's blood. That would be a dream come true for me. I should have just jumped at her and sucked her blood while her eyes were closed. It was too much for me to handle. Her blood was too much, and it smelled too dangerous in a good way.

I was such a tease, and it made Bellduh shiver. I lost myself as I danced for Bellduh. I was craving her blood so bad. I thought that if Bellduh had let me taste some of her blood, I would not have been able to stop.

I finally finished my romantic, lusty dance. As soon as I finished, Bellduh applauded.

We were on my bed, and we just sat there and had small talk. It seemed too early in our relationship to even kiss. She could have kissed me at any time, but she doesn't.

We had spent the rest of the time just talking about school and some other weird stuff. We have a great time together.

My dad was rarely home. I was used to my dad coming home really late. Sometimes he was out for days. He loved the outdoors. Bellduh and I stayed up really late and spent the rest of my night on the couch. I never slept, but I still liked to close my eyes and dream.

I missed the days where I actually used to sleep. It must have been all the caffeine pills that I've tried. I was normal and wished for a better life. I kind of missed being normal. Bellduh and I moved around from the couch to my bed. We were very indecisive. We played checkers and video games. We went back on my bed and just stared at the ceiling.

Bellduh decided to get her bag, and there was a package that Derek Yucky gave her. Bellduh was too busy thinking about me that she almost forgot about it. I was very curious, so Bellduh opened the package.

There were pictures and a lot of pictures. My mouth dropped. They were frame-by-frame pictures of Bellduh practicing her witchcraft with her friends. She was practicing witchcraft in the nude with her weird friends. What a pervert Derek was.

There was also a note, which Bellduh read:

"Bellduh, I took these pictures and you showed your true self. You really are a wicked witch of the west. What exactly will you do for me now that I have your pictures to show to the world? We are all different, but you and your friends are witches. I tell you what, if you pay me, I will keep your secret safe. By the way, I don't mean pay me with money. I think you get the idea, Bellduh. Your days of putting spells on the town of Eclipse are over."

Yours Truly,

Derek Yucky

This could have ruined Bellduh. Bellduh would have to relocate to avoid the humiliation, and being burned to a crisp. The town of Eclipse looked down on witchcraft. If anyone saw those pictures, Bellduh and her friends were doomed. There was only one thing to do. I had to think very fast.

Derek Yucky had made a big mistake. It was the biggest mistake since sliced bacon. He was going to get paid for sure. I thought about bringing him over to my place for some blood and cheese and act like the whole thing was like no big deal, though Bellduh was a witch.

I was going to take care of the situation since it was critical. Derek Yucky was going to get paid with his own blood. It was time to plan the whole thing out, and I had so much to do before my next manicure.

Derek Yucky was going to pay for his actions. I might have had to tell my dad about the situation since he might have wanted blood. We would have had a drink or two of Derek Yucky's blood that probably tasted like sushi. Yes, it was going to be a feast indeed.

I didn't want this, yet I lived for it and could not wait to have a taste. Bellduh and I just wanted to be left alone so that we could be silly together. I was still a junkie, and I needed to look out for myself. I was a junkie that was just trying to be normal and fit in. Bellduh was also trying to fit in as a person, but she was a wicked witch from the West.

Bellduh decided to stay the night so that we could be silly together. As we relaxed on my bed, we closed our eyes and recited our favorite bible quotes. All I thought about was Bellduh until my head hurt. I loved the peaceful times together.

I hoped that Bellduh had fantasies of me. All I wanted that night was Bellduh to hold me tight. I held her tight, and I hadn't felt so loved in a while.

I was very playful with having Bellduh by my side. I started to smell Bellduh's bloody scent. I looked out the window, and the sky was clear and the stars were romantic.

Bellduh's scent was fresh and the forest breeze that was just right. Things were peaceful and romantic. Everyone would have envied me because I had what everyone wanted. I enjoyed every moment of Bellduh's bloody scent.

Act 15

The night was long, and I opened my eyes since Bellduh and I had managed to close our eyes and dream. The thunder outside had awakened us. Bellduh and I had decided to discuss our dreams. I told Bellduh to be totally honest with me about her dream. Bellduh told me that she felt so bad that she had a special craving for someone familiar to me. She had to admit that she couldn't help but dream of my distant cousin that she had never met. Sir Carsmile Cuddles was my distant cousin from an unknown land, and I was a little disappointed, but not surprised since he was a Cuddles.

I wondered how Bellduh could have known about my distant cousin. I had no idea since Bellduh was weird. Bellduh probably wondered what it would have been like to have him romance her to death. Her spells must have triggered her imagination. The night was young, and I craved Bellduh's blood immediately. Bellduh and I closed our eyes. She wanted to tell me what she had dreamt of. Bellduh began to tell me about her dream...

She found herself in Sir Carsmile Cuddle's home. I was not there. The living room was romantic and misty. She decided to take my hand, and she used a spell to show me what she saw and felt. She was in a very large room with a piano, candle light, and large bed with a silk spread nearby, and there was a table of hot chocolate with marshmallows melting down. There was also a monkey nearby. I didn't see any cheese or crackers.

The room was filled with a light mist that surrounded Bellduh. She could somehow smell my distant cousin's amazing scent. He was near, and Bellduh's blood smelled divine to him. He came closer to her, which made me rather uncomfortable.

She wondered if he would give her a massage with his large hands. She hoped that he gave her a massage to remember and wanted to make out with him.

Bellduh wanted him to take her hand and kiss it. She watched as he walked slowly out of the mist and walked to her. He was dressed in an expensive looking suit. He was dressed to drink.

He had a bottle of blood accompanied by two wine glasses. He had very good taste. He confronted Bellduh with his seductive face and perfect hair, but it wasn't as perfect as mine, yet it was a nice effort. Sir Carsmile Cuddles told Bellduh how he wanted her from the start. Since the first time their eyes met, he was amazed at Bellduh's mysterious ways. I had no idea where they had met before. I was suspicious that Bellduh had dreamt of him before. He told Bellduh that he thought about her and her beautiful scent. He had been waiting for Bellduh to come into the tanning salon so that she could tan that pale skin of hers. He wanted to examine every part of her body. I thought that was like so weird.

Bellduh fell for my distant cousin's kind words in a heartbeat. She was more beautiful than he had remembered.

Bellduh asked about his piano that was in the room.

He didn't mean to brag, but as a matter of fact, yes, it was his piano. He had originally bought it for another woman, but he wanted to wait for Bellduh to find him. A monkey had come out to play the piano as they started to dance together as if they were in a dance contest.

Bellduh actually had never had the pleasure of dancing foolishly with another guy. I hated every second of it. She wanted to learn though, and she didn't care that she looked like a clown.

Sir CarsmileCuddles took her hand and took Bellduh to the dance floor. They danced side by side, and he smiled at her. I watched in disgust. Sir Carsmile Cuddles was my enemy, not my distant cousin.

He told Bellduh to dance for him. He wanted to watch her play the piano. He had some sort of fetish for girls and pianos.

Bellduh refused at first since she had no experience at all and did not want to disappoint him.

He told Bellduh that he wanted to hear her call him Carsmile. He told her to give the piano a try.

She agreed that she could do that. She asked him not to laugh at her since she was so nervous and sweaty.

He told Bellduh to begin playing the piano. He was excited to hear Bellduh play. He was as giddy as a happy dog.

Bellduh nervously started to play the piano. At first, her fingers rattled, but then she started to get the hang of it. She had no idea what type of tune she was playing, but he loved it, but I thought that he was just being polite so that he could suck on Bellduh's blood.

She told him that she thought she was horrible and that she would put a spell on him if he laughed at her. She felt that her piano sounded like a cat screaming in agony. She quickly looked at Sir Carsmile Cuddles, and he was obviously holding in his laughter. I tried not to giggle, though I was certain that Bellduh would not put an evil spell on me. I had my right hand covering my mouth. Bellduh was blushing like a tomato since she knew that I found the whole thing humorous.

She could tell that she was a joke. Bellduh was so embarrassed that she just wanted to run away. She hoped that everything would be fine.

Bellduh continued to play for him. Her piano playing had suddenly sounded more like a screaming baby. Sir Carsmile Cuddles stopped Bellduh from further humiliating herself. He grabbed her hands from further contaminating the piano.

He placed his arms around her and placed his hands on Bellduh. She stopped playing the piano for eternity. He gave Bellduh a smile as she gazed into his red eyes.

He told her that her piano playing was memorable in a bad way. Bellduh wanted to continue playing for him, but he told her the truth. He told Bellduh that she was horrible and that she was not to look at a piano ever again. Bellduh still adored him.

He showed Bellduh how he loved to dance while the piano was being played.

The monkey began to play his piano as she watched every moment while he danced in his underwear. She kept an eye on his muscular body as he danced the night away.

She thought he was very romantic. She watched his eyes, his lips and watched every step he took. There was a lot of passion in Sir Carsmile Cuddles.

Bellduh wanted to kiss him right then and there. My mouth had watered with jealousy. She wanted him to tear her clothes off and make love to her on the piano as the monkey watched. That was a weird fetish indeed. I supposed that witches were just weird.

It started to thunderstorm, but the mood was still romantic and peaceful. My distant cousin could smell Bellduh's blood, which smelled like freshly baked lasagna.

He continued to entertain Bellduh as she adored him. He began to juggle bananas as if he was entertaining Bellduh in some sort of a freak show. The monkey applauded when he was done his foolish act. After he had finished, he carried her to the large bed nearby. They relaxed on the bed, and he was gazing deep into Bellduh's eyes. He ran his fingers around her neck and touched her hair as she touched his impressive hair.

He kissed her around the neck and made his way to her lips, and their mouths were locked with passion as I watched in agony. The monkey was making a video of the whole thing. The monkey also seemed to have noticed me and offered me a banana, but I kindly declined. Sir Carsmile Cuddles started to take her clothes off her body, and my mouth watered with eagerness.

His hands on Bellduh filled my mind with dirty thoughts of bloody milkshakes with whipped cream on top. I didn't mind treating myself to junk food once in a while, though I was watching my figure. I knew that I couldn't really ruin my figure, but I liked to think like a normal person, since it was one of the steps of fitting in. Bellduh enjoyed the whole thing way too much for my liking. Things were getting too hot for me to handle. He happened to have a bottle of scented massage oil that he wanted to use on Bellduh. He told her to get comfortable so that he could blow on her and massage her body. My distant cousin had some nerve. He took the bottle of oil and let the oil drip all over Bellduh's ravishing body.

It tickled her at first, and I found it funny. He started to run his hands on her upper neck area. His hands slowly made their way down, with his fingers pressing gently. His hands massaged her lower back, and he moved his hands up and down her back area. His strong hands made their way down to her butt, as he squeezes her cheeks. He started to massage the back of Bellduh's thighs and moved his hands slowly in every direction.

After a soothing back massage, I wanted one for myself since it looked very tempting. He asked Bellduh to turn around so he could massage her front side. She slowly turned, and she was now on her back. Bellduh had a lot of chest hair. I guessed it was genetic. Sir Carsmile Cuddles took the oil bottle and let the oil drip on her body. She smiled as he started to massage her upper body. She closed her eyes as he began. He started to rub her neck gently and made his way down to her private area. He rubbed them delicately and made his way slowly down to her legs. His hands rubbed her legs. He placed one leg at a time up over his shoulder as he massaged them. After massaging her legs, he then started with a foot massage.

Bellduh felt like she was in Heaven. He knew exactly how to use his hands. Every move was perfect, and the timing was flawless. I did my best to learn from the master. He started to massage her private area with his tongue. He must have studied the art of gynecology. He was that good at what he did. He used his whole mouth on Bellduh's private part.

Bellduh said to him that he could have her for breakfast, lunch, dinner, and dessert. He was really amazing at pleasing her. He was very passionate. He kissed Bellduh all around while she grabbed his almost perfect hair with her hands as he continued to help himself to Bellduh. They switched positions, and he continued on Bellduh. He was like royalty according to Bellduh.

He was all over Bellduh. He made sweet passionate love to her while the monkey and I watched on in envy. He was a professional love maker with his lips and hands. He could have given a lot of guys some tips on how to make love. After having passionate moments together, they stayed in bed holding each other. I couldn't believe that it was over so soon. It seemed to end just like that. The romance between Sir Carsmile Cuddles and Bellduh stayed in my mind forever. I wondered if Bellduh would ever be the same.

Act 16

Puppy Chow

Jacub was not around school much. I heard a rumor that he had been turned into a puppy. I wondered if Bellduh's friends had anything to do with it. I started to worry about Jacub. I wondered if he was eating puppy chow. I did have some feelings for him. I was a junkie, but not really a monster. I still cared somewhat about others. Jacub may have been different, but he was still a person and had feelings. I hadn't even seen his friends around either. I didn't care that much about them. I was more interested in Jacub. He might not have even been in Eclipse for all that I knew.

I wondered if he was on some sort of vacation. He could have been in a dog pound. I hoped that he was not captured. I wondered where in the world Jacub would go on vacation. The town of Eclipse just didn't feel the same without Jacub and his little gang.

The day had finally ended. I made my way home, and I could see Jacub across from me. He was waiting for me, as I walked in the dark forest, and it suddenly started to rain.

I wondered why Jacub was waiting for me. He looked kind of silly as a puppy. I knew it was him, and the rumors were true. He still smelled nasty as usual. That was not a surprise since Jacub had the worst hygiene in Eclipse.

That day he carried a different scent, like blue cheese with garlic sauce, onion rings, and fried chicken. It was an interesting combination. He didn't look happy to see me even if he had a puppy face.

"Jacub! Where have you been hiding?" I asked.

"I know what you are, Edworth! You and your family are junkies from that circus freak show. I came here to tell you to stay away from Bellduh. Witches and junkies don't belong together. Does she even know about you?"

"Of course she does. Stay away from Bellduh? Why? What are you talking about?"

"Listen here, Edworth, my uncle told me about your unusual kind. I believe the two of you have met. His name is Silly Blacky. He told me everything! You used to be in the circus freak show. Look, I know what you are, and I came here to bully you and to tell you to stay the hell away from Bellduh. She isn't like you. Don't underestimate me, Edworth. My kind may stink, but we're not stupid. Edworth, if you come onto our property again, we will egg your home."

"Did Bellduh turn you into a puppy?"

"Don't make fun of me, Edworth! You are a junkie! You are the epitome of evil! You are so mean! Don't worry, Edworth, I won't tell anyone about you. Why are you even in school? It's not like you need to learn anything. You are a true bloodsucker. You have no business even socializing with normal people. This business is not over between us. You will be seeing more and more of my kind. Keep away from Bellduh. Stay out of Eclipse High. You should just leave Eclipse if you know what's best."

I was truly shocked to hear Jacub talk to me like that. It hurt my feelings.

"After all the things I've done for you, Jacub, this is the respect I get? I was about to offer to buy you some puppy treats, but that deal is off!"

"Things are different now. You fooled me once with your beauty and made we want to be just like you, Edworth, but now I have seen the light. Being turned into a puppy has changed me."

"My kind are all part of a puppy pack now that the curse has been put on us. We may not be strong, but together we pack a strong stink!"

I giggled at Jacub.

"There is nothing funny here, Edworth! Don't laugh at me, there is nothing funny about my kind!"

Jacub was such a joke. I actually felt really bad for him and his kind. His little cute puppy pack were pathetic. I always wanted a puppy. The only thing was that I wouldn't have been able to handle the stink of Jacub. He was a true repellent. At least he had a gift for self-defense.

"You made your point, Jacub. If you don't mind, I would like to be on my way home. I'm thirsty you know, and a man's got to drink."

"Remember what I told you, Edworth. You've been warned. This will not be the last time I see you."

"Until we meet again, Jacub."

"Edworth, trust me, we will see each other again."

Jacub barked at me and finally went away. I made my way home.

My dad was not home. There were so many questions I have for him. Too much was going on. I went on the couch and stared at the fire. I was worried, and I didn't know what to do next. I was bothered by the big question that haunted me. I wondered when I was going to turn Bellduh into a junkie like me. That was the only way we could be together forever and ever.

Act 17

Guess What I Am

I planned to confront Bellduh and hoped to turn her into what I was. I was a junkie, and that was life. I couldn't take the suffering anymore. The whole thing was getting out of hand. We needed to be open if anything was going to work. Keeping secrets from each other was not going to help improve our relationship. It was just making my life worse. The town of Eclipse was just full of surprises. Nothing really surprised me anymore. I embraced everything that came my way.

The longer Bellduh and I waited; the harder things would be. I wondered if Bellduh could be as open as I could. It would have been the best way to go. I was good at influencing people, so I was going to do my best to make things go the way I wanted them to.

School was going along as usual. Nothing special was going on that day. I confronted Bellduh in the cafeteria.

I told her to meet me in the dark forest, and she agreed that it was a great idea.

School was out, and I didn't go home. I went straight to our meeting area in the dark forest. I waited there until it was time.

I slowly looked up to see Bellduh as she stood across from me. She looked like she had a million questions for me. She walked closer to me as she looked at a dead bear on the ground. She knew that I hurt the bear and tasted it.

"That was animal cruelty you know!" Bellduh yelled.

"What do you think I am? I think it's pretty obvious, Bellduh. Just say it. Tell me what I am. Say it. What am I? I want to hear you say the words, like right now; you witch!"

"What did you call me? Judging by the blood, you're an animal abuser."

"Bellduh, is that your best guess?"

"Well, if you are not, then what?"

I told Bellduh to turn around and close her eyes while I pulled my glitter container out and sprinkled it on my skin. I sparkled like the stars at night. Bellduh slowly opened her eyes.

"No way! Seriously? That's like so beautiful, Edworth. You must be an angel, right?"

"Keep guessing, Bellduh. I got all night."

"Edworth, are you crazy?"

"Please calm down, Bellduh. I will tell you what I am, but you need to just take a deep breath."

She took a deep breath, and she ran her fingers through her hair in confusion.

"Edworth, I'm ready for the truth. Tell me right now. What are you? I promise that whatever you say, I will be ok with it. Just tell me."

"Bellduh, please don't hate me. Bellduh, I'm like… well, I'm a junkie. Do you know what that means?"

Bellduh's mouth dropped. She walked back slowly.

"A junkie? Tell me something I don't know, Edworth. Like, I knew that. I just hate that you have to hurt animals."

I tried not to laugh. I let out an innocent smirk.

"Well, are you ok, Bellduh? I mean, it gets better you know."

"I'm fine, Edworth. It's cool; I'm cool. Nevertheless, there has to be another way for you to drink blood.

"Let's get some things out of the way. Ask me some junkie questions. I'm willing to answer any kinds of questions that you have for me. I can only imagine how you must be feeling right now."

"Yes, we should talk about what you are since we never really did cover that area, Edworth."

"Go ahead Bellduh, ask me anything you want, I can take it."

"How old are you, Edworth?"

"Too old for you. In fact, I'm way too old for you."

"Well, how long have you been too old for me?"

"Wouldn't you like to know, Bellduh."

"I didn't know junkies lived that long. Have you ever killed anyone before? Have you ever killed any witches?"

"Yes, but they were all jerks. Witches? Yes, they deserved to die. I sucked their blood out, and I liked it. I heard some junkies sparkle in the sunlight, but I don't sparkle. I had to go to the art store to buy sparkles and sprinkle them on me just to look cool in front of you. However, I can glow in the dark when the full moon is out, and it is like so neat."

"Wow, glow in the dark during a full moon. I want to see that sometime, Edworth. Would you ever like... go out for a burger with me?"

"Yes, I would love that, Bellduh. I'm also a virgin."

"Well, I'm like a virgin too, so maybe we could like be virgins together."

"That sounds like a plan, Bellduh."

"I actually like extra virgin olive oil, Edworth. I use a lot of that oil in my witchcraft experiments. It's like so cool."

Bellduh smiled. She seemed to like our meeting together. Breaking the ice helped our cause.

"So, you're like really a witch? You and your friends?"

"Edworth, you are something. So, where do we go from here? You know people are going to talk about us more if we get serious. Like, really talk."

"Let them. I don't really care. So, would you like to go for some Chinese food, Bellduh?"

"Sure, I'd like that."

Bellduh and I started to really get along. I walked her to my place. We sat by the fire, and we told each other stories.

It was a great night for us. A junkie couldn't have asked for anything more that night. I loved that night so much. We took turns making up bad puppy jokes regarding Jacub.

Jacub smelled so bad; his own mother didn't want anything to do with him, and she probably stunk pretty bad herself.

Nothing made me happier than being with Bellduh. It was breathtaking. Bellduh and I enjoyed the rest of our night, and we cherished our time together. Hours went by, and we made our way to my bed.

It was storming outside, and the thunder was very loud. I went to my bed, and I looked forward to holding Bellduh. I closed my eyes, and it felt great. The night was still young, and Bellduh was about to fall asleep. Bellduh's scent was for real, and it felt like a dream. I wondered why the smell was so tempting.

Act 18

The day was beautiful and cloudy. It was just the way I loved it. I hated the sun with a passion since it burned my skin and my eyes. If I could have blocked out the sun for good, I would have. Mother Nature hated me, and that was a fact. I always knew that she did. I had a big smile on my face and for a good reason. My life felt more complete than ever before. Bellduh completed me. Having Bellduh in my life was the most wonderful feeling.

I got up and prepared for school. I made my way out, and I was on my way to school. I took my time just like I usually did.

Bellduh waited for me in the schoolyard. She smiled and took my hand. We were big time at Eclipse High. Someone should have sounded the bells and rolled out the red carpet. We walked hand in hand.

Everyone was outside today. That was the moment people practical loved being at Eclipse High. They saw us together, and they also looked forward to the drama, gossip, and pure excitement. I waited for the paparazzi to arrive. We were like celebrities at Eclipse High.

Kermit saw me and gave me a great big smile. I could tell he was nothing but happy for me. I saw him with Roosilly, who kind of looked like she was jealous of me. I loved it, and I hoped that she was jealous.

I loved making other people jealous. She should have been jealous because I was Edworth Cuddles, the hottest junkie at Eclipse High. I looked at Roosilly and smiled, but Roosilly rolled her eyes back at me and looked away.

I saw Derek Yucky. He was so sneaky, and he was evil. What a complete jerk he was. I disliked him so much.

Bellduh's weird friends were nothing but smiles. Every person at school was staring at us, including the faculty. I loved the attention, and so did Bellduh. I was like an attention whore.

Whatever I wanted I got. We made it safely inside the school and went to our own classes. The whole day was nothing but stares and rumors. I could hear whispers and jokes.

However, I wasn't a joke; everyone else was a joke. I was madly in love. Bellduh was mine, and no one could have her but me. I went to Chemistry class, and even the teacher knew what was going on. Casper looked at me and smiled, and he was very sincere in his feelings.

I could not even concentrate in class. Casper made onion jokes all day. We would giggle the whole class. In music class, Bellduh and I would play our duets together, and we were on top of the class.

Some were jealous, and some people were happy to see us in love. Not all of my other classes were with Bellduh, but people still kept up the dirty birdy rumors.

The rumors were ridiculous, like, oh I heard Bellduh is pregnant. Another rumor was like; oh, I heard Edworth is cheating on Bellduh.

The rumors had spread like wildfire. Other rumors were that I was gay, and another was that I was cheating on Bellduh with Roosilly. Even Casper managed to end up in the rumors.

After the lunch break had ended, we all went to our classes. The rest of the day was typical. I was supposed to walk Bellduh home, but she had detention for telling some girl off in class that was starting up all kinds of rumors. Bellduh had threatened to cast a spell on them.

One cold night, I took Bellduh out to the movies. We caught a chick flick. It was some cheesy vampire movie. I was a true gentleman. I bought the movie tickets, and Bellduh bought the popcorn and pop, all for herself, of course. We made our way to the middle of the theater. The movie started, and I placed my arm around her. She ate popcorn with extra butter. It stunk, and it ruined the moment, but I loved Bellduh's blood, so I tolerated it.

The movie was so cheesy and was probably the worst movie ever made. I guessed Bellduh thought I would like it. I just wanted to spend time with her as much as possible. That's what really mattered to me. I started to lean in on Bellduh to kiss her. I could taste the foul popcorn and butter on her lips. This was such a big mistake. I hoped that I never had to take her to the movies ever again. Maybe she could have just not ordered the popcorn because it was like so gross. Well, it was still great being with her. I watched Bellduh as the movie went on. I stared into her eyes and watched as she laughed at the cheesy moments of the movie. I admired her hair and ran my hand through her beautiful hair. She looked at me and smiled as her almost perfect heavenly white teeth sparkled in my eyes.

The girls around me were nothing but jealous of Bellduh. I could see the hate in their eyes as I touched Bellduh. I could smell their blood boiling around me. It really smelled great. Going to the movies had turned out to be a good idea. The bloody smells had managed to overpower the foul smell of popcorn and butter.

The night was going smoothly. I also thought that I would bring Bellduh here more often just to make all the girls jealous. That was pretty fun. The movie was coming close to the end. The only thing I hated was the fact that the date would be over soon. I looked forward to many more nights like it. I loved watching how happy Bellduh was with me. I loved seeing that side of her. She was very different when she was with me. I wondered if she would ever be a junkie like me. We would have to just wait and see what happened.

Act 19

My dad and I sat by the fire. My dad started to reminisce about his time with the Voltweety. He mentioned that the Voltweety were part of a circus act that was a freak show, not that there is anything wrong with that. They took their acts all around the world. They were the worst junkies of them all. You would have never found a larger circus act of junkies than the Voltweety.

The Voltweety supported junkies all around the world. My dad admitted that he was once part of the circus act, but then he changed.

The Voltweety loved the circus. They had many talents to show. Some things they did were unspeakable. Their acts were so horrendous that my dad would not speak of them.

The Voltweety wanted nothing but to live in peace, but that was hard to believe. They had done many horrible acts to other junkies that had better circus acts than they did. They continued to do many unthinkable acts against other junkies.

The Voltweety liked to keep their circus acts secretive. They were very low profile. They were a silent but deadly freak show.

The Voltweety were the most conceited junkies in the world. Some of their names were Farse, Crackass, Cactus, Farse's cousin Pulpfixia, and Crackass's cousin Assawhora.

The really powerful junkies of the Voltweety were named Eatmee, Pain and the most paranoid, Panic.

Farse was one of the circus leaders. Pain and Panic followed him. Eatmee loved eating cats and sucking the blood right out. Eatmee was a really passionate junkie. Pain loved to inflict a lot of torture on other junkies by tickling them. Pain really loved her fetishes. There was nothing more exciting to Pain than watching others suffer. Pain was a very sick and twisted junkie.

It was usually a bloody ordeal when Pain was around. As for Panic, this junkie was the most paranoid junkie that existed. When Panic got too nervous, a lot of smelly gas was involved. It could happen where Panic was near.

It was very difficult to describe how paranoid Panic was. Even the other Voltweety members got a little nervous around Panic. One day my dad made love to a female junkie. It was the most extraordinary thing he had ever experienced.

It was then he decided that he was sick of being part of the freak show. It really wasn't for him anymore. It was a painful experience. Unfortunately, the Voltweety did not approve his decision and wanted him destroyed.

One night he escaped the Voltweety and then he was hunted. He was saddened by the slavery of his lover Shiarax. She was captured and forced to be in the circus. The Voltweety tickled Shiarax's body until she went crazy. They humiliated her, where other junkies could see and be afraid. My dad had finally found a peaceful place in the world, but had to move every few years.

Finally, our current home was in the town of Eclipse. This was where we belonged, and we were here to stay. My Dad and I spent the rest of our evening by the fire. It was a great night for telling stories. We never ran out of them. My dad and I have been together for many decades. We had enough stories to last many more decades to come.

Act 20

Beers and Smiles

The morning had arrived, and I was out in the dark forest. The rain started, and I had the biggest craving that morning for a big fat bear. I was very thirsty that morning, so I made my way deep into the dark forest. There was not an animal in sight. That was unusual, and I wondered where all of them could have been.

I heard a crackle from behind me. I turned, and the stranger that stood behind was a junkie.

"Sorry, I didn't mean to scare you," he said.

"Looks like I'm not alone in Eclipse. Where did you come from? What's your name?" I asked.

"No, I've been here a while. I'm Smiley Beers. Pleasure to meet you."

"I'm Edworth Cuddles. You seem to smile a lot. Have been drinking? My family and I have been in Eclipse for ages."

Smiley Beers happened to be another junkie. Just when I thought I was alone with my family, I was wrong. He had curly red hair, dark, disturbing eyes, and smiled a lot. He was kind of creepy. I wondered if he had been drinking beer since junkies don't usually drink. Drinking was against our junkie policy. I was getting bad vibes from him already. He looked at me like he wanted something from me. I was going to soon find out. One of the rules I had in life was to never trust a strange junkie. That was one rule I had always kept.

"Edworth Cuddles, that's a pretty name. You must be worth something, and you must cuddle a lot, right?"

He offered his hand, and I shook his hand in disgust. His face was completely happy with a big smile. What a creeper.

"What brings you to these parts, Smiley? Do you live close by?"

"I live in a cabin on the other side of town. I thought I would see if anything interesting was out in this dark forest. Now I know there is. Have you caught any normal people? I thought I would drink something. I was also thinking of joining the freak show."

"My family and I don't feed off the blood of normal people anymore. We found it barbaric to do so. I can show you there are a lot of bears around these parts. You shouldn't speak of the freak show since it is forbidden."

Smiley smiled at me.

"Really… You don't feed off the blood of normal people. You are a crazy junkie. That is fascinating. You're a junkie, and you should do it. Drinking animals is no fun anymore. There is a local high school nearby. We should lure them in one by one. We can really take this town of Eclipse."

Smiley Beers obviously was not a good listener. Either that or he was disrespectful. I tried to reason with him. He was one stubborn junkie.

"I'm sorry, Smiley, I don't swing that way anymore. It is against policy. I actually attend Eclipse High. You should probably look elsewhere. Your strange kind is not welcome here, and you drink beer."

Smiley looks surprised, yet he still smiled.

"Really? You attend Eclipse High. You are one of them? Trying to be like them, Edworth? You want to be like a normal person. They are not like us, Edworth. We are junkies, and we belong to the freak show. The Voltweety will not like that if they ever find out about you. You will be hunted down and humiliated."

"That's the life I've chosen. I think it would be best if you left the town of Eclipse. If you are tasting normal people, you can't do that around here unless you have a fair reason, and you drink beer."

"Have you killed any normal people lately, Edworth?"

I hesitated. This might have been a big mistake. Smiley Beers appeared to be clever. He knew right away that I have killed a normal person, yet I just didn't want to share that information. See, I was really thirsty, and he was kind of a bad person. I knew he could sense the blood of a normal person that still lurked on me.

Smiley approached me. He was too close to me and made me uncomfortable. He sniffed me and exhaled. He smiled, and I knew he was going to tell me how good I smelled.

"Edworth, you have been a very bad junkie. I smell sweet blood on you, and it smells good. Why are you holding back on me? I want some too. I'm sick of drinking beer and smiling all the time."

"You got me, Smiley. Please try to understand that I was thirsty, and you drink beer, so that is much worse than my crime."

"I didn't mean to drink beer. I smile a lot; I know that. I still want to drink the blood, and I want it now."

"She was rather tasty. I admit; she was a feast. Are you happy now? You will have to stop drinking beer and find your own blood."

"Well, I am glad you admit to what you have done. There is no shame in it. This was a rather interesting. You should think about what I said about taking this town of Eclipse. I will be on my way. I will see you again, Edworth. I will bring back some beer because I like it, and you should try it. I smile too much, but too much is better than too little."

Smiley walked away and took his beer breath and smiley face with him.

I walked into Spanish class, though I was not really a fan of Spanish class. I could never learn the language that well. I was pretty basic when it came to speaking and understanding.

I would have loved to learn French or Italian. Those languages seemed like the language of love. Roosilly sat across from me; Alicia sat on my right, and Rebecca sat in front of me. We had a few minutes before class started up. I was really not in the mood for their shenanigans. I could feel the rumors and gossip time approaching.

"Ola! Ola! Edworth!" Rebecca shouted.

"Ola Edworth," Alicia said.

"Hey, I see you've all been beefing up on your Spanish," I said.

"Edworth, how are you and Bellduh working out? I see things are pretty tight with the two of you," Roosilly said.

I tried to handle the situation with clarity and peacefulness.

"Things are just fine, thanks for asking."

"There you have it Roosilly! All is well in the love department!" Rebecca shouted.

"In other news, that new kid with the weird hair has run away from home and has been declared missing. The cops are going to every house asking questions," Roosilly said.

"Wow, that's like, horrible news. Why would that kid runaway from home?" Alicia asked.

"I heard that kid was really into something deep. I heard she was doing drugs. She was dealing too. I also heard she was into some crazy other stuff," Roosilly said.

"Like… who told you that?" Rebecca asked.

"A little bird told me. Who cares? It's just some rumor going around," Roosilly said.

"Well, maybe she was into some bad stuff, but she didn't seem like a bad kid. She probably lost her head and wanted to see what's out there. I'm sure she will pop up again around here," I said.

The truth was that Smiley Beers was thirsty and took the kid and had too much of her blood to drink, but I didn't want to get involved. I found out since I knew all and smelled all.

The Spanish teacher walked into the classroom. The class began, and the teacher started the class off by explaining that a fellow student had been away and that if anyone had seen her should have reported to the principal's office immediately.

They would never find the kid with the weird hair.

Act 22

Puppy Names

One night, Bellduh and I had decided to have a picnic in the dark forest. Bellduh wanted a puppy of her own, and we had decided to think of a name for it. We enjoyed drinking red grape juice and some cheese and cracker, though I was not fond of any of it. I had decided that I would buy Bellduh a puppy, and she was excited about it since she could not afford one.

"You do know that you would have to feed the puppy and walk it daily, Bellduh. A puppy is not a toy. You should name the puppy when you get it. I know that puppies already have names, but we should come up with our own name for it."

"This is all so new to me, Edworth. Having a puppy is like being a mother. I would love it so much until the day I die; I swear."

"No matter what happens, you don't dare put a spell on the poor puppy, Bellduh. That's not cool at all. So what's on your mind about naming the puppy?"

"There are so many names I'd like to name my puppy, Edworth. I don't even know where to start. How about Sherri?"

"Sherri sounds cute. How about something else? I think you should start with Annabelle?"

That sounds so old fashion, Edworth. I don't know about Anabelle. There are just so many names to choose from."

"Why are we even naming the puppy by a girl's name? Do we even know whether it will be a boy or a girl?"

"You do have a point, Edworth, but let's choose a girl's name first before we move onto a boy's name. How does Shea sound?

"What are you serious right now? Shea? Is that even a name?

"Edworth, anything can be a name if you decided it is a name."

"Well, how does the name Rosa sound?"

"It sounds so Italian. Is the puppy going to be Italian?

"So we're arguing about countries now?"

"No, I just think it sounds so Italian. Like, the puppy isn't going to be in a gang. So let's try to think of something decent."

I wish that I had never decided to get Bellduh, a puppy. I quivered in disgust at how irritating Bellduh had become over puppy names. Bellduh was such a witch, if you know what I mean.

"Bellduh, I think you should decide on naming the puppy yourself. It would be much easier, don't you think?"

"You're involved whether you like it or not, you junkie."

"So, now I'm a junkie. Well, you're a witch."

"Give me a break, Edworth. Just help me come up with some names if you really care about me."

"Well, you leave me no choice, Bellduh. Let me think of something that you will love. How about you name the puppy Rositta?"

"Were you Italian in your past life, Edworth?"

"So, not good enough. I think I know what you want to name your puppy. A good name would be Ramsay."

"Please stop, Edworth. This whole puppy naming thing is not helping at all."

"Like I said before this whole thing should be your decision, Bellduh. It's your puppy, so you can decide when I get you the puppy. Trust me. The name will just come naturally to you when you get him or her."

"That sounds fair enough, Edworth. You do have a point."

"That's fine, Bellduh. Well, at least we didn't think anything dumb to name the puppy. We could have come up with plenty of ridiculous names like, Ratmee, Rattree, Beatree, Roobetree, or like, Renezmea. All dumb names in my opinion."

"Edworth, you are like so funny. You really are a junkie. Where would you come up with such dumb names like those? That was so made up and ridiculous. You're lucky I don't put a spell on you, Edworth."

Bellduh was right about the names. They were so not intelligent at all and truly ridiculous. I had learned my lesson to never get into puppy names unless I wanted to feel the wrath of Bellduh.

Act 23

Class ended, and I made my way out. I walked through the school halls. It was a long crappy day, and I was on my way to meet Bellduh. Bellduh had left me a note. She was so sneaky.

I read the note:

"Edworth, open and read it at the dark forest."

Bellduh wanted me to open it when I arrived at the dark forest, but I didn't want to wait. I wondered what it was.

I made my way to the dark forest. I wondered if Bellduh would have considered being a junkie. I think she wanted to talk about becoming a junkie.

I believed that I tempted her into becoming one. No one could resist. Bellduh would have loved being a junkie like me.

I wondered what she really wanted to talk about. She probably wanted to tell me that she loved me. I wondered how she would say it. I began to imagine how Bellduh would tell me that she loved me.

As long as she said I love you, I guessed that it was something, and it was better than nothing. As long as she said the words, that's all that mattered.

It meant at least something if she had said the words. I was really sensitive on the subject.

I waited in the dark forest. It was a nice and peaceful. Suddenly, it started to rain. I imagined myself proposing to Bellduh. I could have just imagined what our wedding day would be like.

Bellduh would have been in her perfect white wedding dress. She would have waited for her dad to walk her down. My beautiful wedding would have been held in the dark forest. The skies would have been blue, and the birds would have been chirping.

I would not have wanted any rain on my wedding day. Everyone would have been there for my wedding day.

Jacub would have stood with his kind on one side and everyone else on the other side. Even in my imagination, Jacub still stunk horribly. I had to admit it was hard to imagine a Jacub that didn't stink.

The other guests would have been on the other side to accommodate them from the smelly puppies.

Bellduh would have looked perfect, absolutely perfect. I never would have seen her so dolled up. She would have had a great big smile. Her eyes would have sparkled and would have stood out above everyone and anything.

I opened Bellduh's letter:

"Dear Edworth,

I'm excessively shy to say these words in person, so I had to write them from the heart. This letter I write is for your beautiful eyes only.

Before you and I decide to go any further in our little fairy tale, I want to open up, like really open up about the real me. By the time you finish reading this letter, you will may decide to leave the dark forest, but if you are still there waiting for me, I know that you are willing to forgive me, tolerate me, and go even further than ever before. Not one person in Eclipse has ever experienced the relationship we have. I know I can be like such a witch sometimes. The truth is, every single day I think of you. The first time you set foot at Eclipse High, I knew you would be mine. Your lovely heavenly perfect hair and pretty delicate pale face just fascinate me. Your innocent looking eyes are heavenly. I don't care if you're a junkie.

Your red soft lips touching mine can stay locked forever. When I touch you Edworth, your coldness is a little hard to get used to but you're hot. I just have to admit that you're sweet and perfect. There is something sweet about you. That would be cool if we would like actually be the same temperature. It would be like so cool. You must love that idea; I bet. If we were ever to be together forever, I wonder if you would be able to tolerate me in the morning. I like to spend a lot of time on my hair in the morning. I have to make sure my makeup is just right. I love looking at myself in the mirror. I spend even more time putting on my makeup. I find it makes me prettier. I whiten my teeth with strips; it really works. I only buy the best clothes, and I get manicures when it's time.

Girls have to do what girls have to do. I guess you can say I am very high maintenance. I wonder if I will have to worry about any of that if I become like you. I love it when our eyes meet, Edworth. You suck the life right out of me. Your butt is nice and firm. That's a butt to die for. A lot of girls want to slap that butt of yours.

When my hot skin touches your cold body, it makes me shiver. It's a real rush. Together, we are the perfect couple. All the girls wish they were me. It's really true. If only I could read your mind, Edworth. I would love to be able to get inside your head. What are you really thinking, Edworth? Some things are best left to the imagination. Whatever you decide will either haunt me forever or make me the happiest girl in Eclipse. Just remember, I will always be there for you. I won't ever forget about you. I will be the shoulder you can place your head on. I mean, if you decide you just want to be friends, I'm fine with that. Well, I will actually turn you into a frog. Well, this is it. I leave you now until we meet. I will always love you.

I'm always your witch,"

Bellduh.

After reading that letter, I decided one thing.

Bellduh Swansinner was a total weirdo. Truthfully, after reading that letter, it didn't matter. Bellduh's beautiful blood was all that mattered to me.

I have never felt so alive in my life with Bellduh. Her scent was what hypnotized me. Her kiss is what completed me, well, it was more her blood. I wanted Bellduh since she was everything I could ever want in a witch. I needed her blood, and I felt weak without it. I would never have let anyone come between us. My decision was made. I wanted to convince her to become like me, a junkie.

She was to be a junkie like me forever. Only time would tell. The wind gently blew through my hair, and it suddenly started to rain.

I wondered where our honeymoon would be. I'm sure Bellduh had some good ideas about where we could travel. I was getting way ahead of myself. I was still waiting for Bellduh to make her way here. The time was getting closer. I was excited, and I could feel my legs shaking. The thought of Bellduh made me shake. I had a feeling that I was not alone here. I could sense movement.

Junkies approached me from across. I had never seen them before. I saw several of them that all dressed the same way. They were wearing pink leotards. It was obvious that they had come from the circus freak show.

"You must be Edworth Cuddles. I have been told so much about you, Edworth. My name is Farse. What a delight it is to meet you."

Farse offered his hand, and I shook it. He had long red hair, obviously the ugliest of them all. He introduced me to his followers, Pain, and Panic.

"Yes. It is a pleasure. Are you part of the Voltweety?" I asked.

"I think you know who we are, Edworth. We know about your dad too. Don't worry Edworth, we are not here for him. We came here for you. You belong to the freak show."

"Rumors spread fast in the junkie world. I know you have been seeing Bellduh Swansinner. Is it true, Edworth? Is her blood as sweet as apple pie?" Farse asked.

"Please don't hurt Bellduh. She is just a helpless wicked witch of the west. She is everything to me. Her blood is beyond words. Why did you come here?" I asked.

"We would very much like to meet this Bellduh Swansinner. You know you can't be with her, Edworth. She is not one of us. She is not a junkie. She is a witch and an evil one. How long did you think this fairy tale would last?" Farse asked.

"I will make her like one of us then. I will change her into a junkie, and we will join the circus. Please trust me."

"Bellduh is coming here right now isn't she? We know this, Edworth. We see all and know all. We will wait for Bellduh to come here, and we will decide her fate," Farse said.

"I was actually just leaving. Bellduh and I are just friends."

"We are not fools, Edworth. If you leave, your dad will pay the consequences by joining the circus and Bellduh will be ours for sure," Farse said.

Suddenly, the greatest smell in the world graced us. Bellduh finally arrived. She looked at the Voltweety and smiled.

"Did you start the party without me? Edworth, aren't you going to introduce me to your friends?" Bellduh asked.

"Farse, this is Bellduh Swansinner. Bellduh, meet the Voltweety. This is Farse, Pain, and Panic."

"So... it is true. Bellduh smells absolutely scrumptious!" Farse murmured.

"You have really dirty minds. Please stop thinking like that. I don't swing that way. I can read minds. It's a rare gift. Please keep your dirty thoughts to yourselves," I said.

"Are you still trying to read minds, Edworth? Come on now, we know you are a fake. If I may, Bellduh, may I have a taste of that beautiful red stuff? I pay top dollar for just a taste you know. What do you say?" Farse asked.

I was embarrassed that the truth about me was out. I was a fake. I couldn't read minds, but I really was good at telling what people were thinking. I could just tell what was on someone's mind, really; you have to believe me.

"Bellduh is not for sale! Stop asking! We will follow your strange rules. Bellduh and I will be together forever and become junkies in love," I said.

"Let's see if Bellduh can feel my wrath," Pain said.

Pain used her power to try tickling Bellduh and succeeded. Bellduh was dying of laughter because she felt like Pain was tickling her. Bellduh was enjoying it.

"This witch is stronger than I thought. I am unable to make her beg for mercy," Pain said.

'What, are you serious? You tried to hurt me? Is that all you have? Seriously? Keep going! That actually felt great!" Bellduh said.

"I don't understand why my power has failed me? This can't be. I feel really weak now. I must go back and regain my strength."

"How excellent! You don't feel Pain's powers. Let's see if you can resist Panic's power," Farse said.

"I'm sorry Farse; I am unable to use my powers on Bellduh. She has some sort of power I can't understand," Panic said.

"Satisfied? Bellduh will make a great junkie! There is no need to test her anymore. We will be together forever," I said.

"Wait, wait. Me? A junkie? When did this happen?" Bellduh said.

"Let me do the talking, Bellduh. These junkies will suck you dry if you don't agree."

"Bellduh, my sweet and lovely Bellduh. You are a real asset to our kind. When is the big day? You and Bellduh must be the same, or we will drink her sweet blood, and you will join the circus freak show. You don't have a choice now," Farse said.

"Really? Great! I never signed up for this. Can I turn back if I change my mind?" Bellduh asked.

"Excuse me? Edworth, your love Bellduh, is not the sharpest witch, is she? Well, at least she smells perfect. She also has a gift," Farse said.

"Hey! I may not be the brightest witch out there, but at least I know what love is. Don't make me cast a spell on all of you," Bellduh said.

Pain and Panic giggled behind Farse.

"Don't make fun of Bellduh. She may be off, sometimes, but she's my girl. She's not the sharpest witch in the West, but she is alright."

"So, it is settled. Bellduh, you and Edworth will have to be junkies together. Don't even think about running away, or we will find you and make you join the town circus. Bellduh, we look forward to seeing you as one of us junkies. Hopefully, you will have a higher I.Q," Farse said.

Pain and Panic giggled. I started to giggle. I couldn't help it since it was kind of fun making fun of Bellduh's I.Q.

"That's not funny," Bellduh said.

"I will make sure Bellduh and I become junkies in love. Please leave us now. We would like to continue with our lives."

"We will leave now, Edworth. We will meet again, and I hope you look forward to being a junkie, Bellduh. Until we meet again," Farse said.

Farse, Pain, and Panic left and went back to where they came from.

Bellduh looked at me disappointed.

"Sorry, Bellduh. If I didn't say all those things, you and I would be in the circus freak show right now. They would make fun of me and send you to be humiliated by other Voltweety. I don't think you want that, do you?"

"That's ok, Edworth. I totally understand. You had to do what was needed, and you stepped up to the plate. I'm proud of you."

"Well, I just don't know if I'm ready to be a junkie like you. If it means keeping you forever, I guess I have to do what I have to do then."

"We have seen many weird things lately. It's only going to get more bizarre. I hope you don't mind," I said.

"I'm glad we're together. Geez, what was up with those weird pink outfits the Voltweety were wearing?" Bellduh asked.

"They really need to get with the fashion program; I wouldn't mind trying on one of those leotards."

"You should give them some tips on fashion, Edworth. They were dressed so cheesy."

"Yes, I should do that. I should take them out shopping. They could use some new threads. That would be something to talk about. I hope we never have to dress like that. They are like so not cool, and I feel bad for Farse. He really sucks."

"What is up with their funny names? They must hate their own names. Their parent must have hated them."

Farse, Pain, and Panic are a mystery, Bellduh. Their parents must have been reading a little too many comic books. Maybe they were trying to start some trend in that junkie thing of theirs. It's very cheesy indeed."

"So, now what, Edworth?"

"I really want to open up to you, Bellduh, in more ways than one. There is just no other way. I hope you can understand how I feel. It hurts so much. I can't get you out of my head, Bellduh. It hurts when I'm away from you. I can stand being without you."

"I'm here, Edworth. That's all that matters."

I go closer and kiss Bellduh passionately.

"Well, I just wanted to tell you something, Bellduh. We have been like really close lately. I just think that it's time that we connect even more."

I had no idea what I was going to tell Bellduh. Things were so unpredictable. I wondered if she really loved a junkie like me. I wondered if she really would have joined me in becoming a junkie. I wondered all sorts of things.

"Edworth, stop teasing me and just say what you want. I really need to hear it. Stop being a douchebag and tell me. Be a junkie!"

I smiled and came right up close to Bellduh and looked deep into her eyes as she looked up at me into my dreamy eyes.

I took her hands with my cold hands, and they were cold since the weather was chilly. I couldn't believe that it was happening. I pulled out a small, cute decorated shoebox. I opened it up, and I showed Bellduh a beautiful, cuddly, teddy bear. I was much too cheap to buy her an expensive ring.

I got on my knees as Bellduh looked directly into my eyes and smiled. I was so nervous. For some strange reason, I felt like I was dreaming. It was really happening, and life was beautiful. I could smell Bellduh's sweet blood calling my name. I wondered how I would fill up my containers with her red honey. I had thought about purchasing Bellduh a broom, but I didn't want her to take it as an insult.

I waited nervously to say my next words. This was the next big step at getting closer to Bellduh's priceless red rum. I've always told her what she wanted to hear, though I cringed at the very words that came out of my mouth. I really longed for her blood, and Bellduh was nothing more but a vessel, but I learned to accept her for more than a wicked witch. I enjoyed romancing the wicked witch of Eclipse. The moment was getting closer as I prepared to make my next move. I raised the teddy bear to Bellduh…

"Bellduh Swansinner, will you be a junkie like me?"

Bellduh's mouth dropped… as I stared deeply—into Bellduh's beautiful witch eyes. Everything was perfect. She stood frozen for several seconds. She didn't say a word…

Printed in Great Britain
by Amazon